CW01374051

Children of the Light

with Best Wishes

by
Karen Wood

authorHOUSE

Karen Wood
x x

AuthorHouse™ UK Ltd.
500 Avebury Boulevard
Central Milton Keynes, MK9 2BE
www.authorhouse.co.uk
Phone: 08001974150

© 2007 Karen Wood. All rights reserved.

No part of this book may be reproduced, stored in a retrieval system, or transmitted by any means without the written permission of the author.

First published by AuthorHouse 10/15/2007

ISBN: 978-1-4343-3894-5 (sc)

Printed in the United States of America
Bloomington, Indiana

This book is printed on acid-free paper.

Acknowledgments

My grateful thanks and acknowledgements go to my lovely partner, Dave, for his unstinting support. Also to Mavis for the way she has encouraged me, and occasionally bullied me, over the years. To Tony and Barbara, who believed in me, sometimes when I didn't believe in myself. To all the lovely people at AuthorHouse of course, without whose help this book would still be dozens of sections piled in a box.

Thank you one and all.

Contents

Acknowledgments v
Introduction ix

Part 1 The Stories

1. Amanda — 3
2. Barry Woodentop — 5
3. Carrie — 9
4. Alicia — 13
5. On The Train — 15
6. Flat On Fire! — 19
7. Goodness Gracious — 23
8. A Night Out With Friends — 25
9. How Are You Doing World? — 29
10. I Didn't Wake Up — 35
11. I Fought In The War — 39
12. I Never Lived On Your Earth — 43
13. I Travelled With My Mother — 47
14. Counting — 51
15. Keep Your Head Down — 53
16. Miranda — 55
17. My Mummy Has Lost Herself — 59
18. Pueblo — 61
19. The Drummer Boy — 65
20. War Torn Countries — 67
21. Biffa's Friend — 69
22. Where Are You? — 71
23. Miriam — 73

24	Bertram	77
25	The Designer	81
26	Marcus	85
27	How Did I End Up Over Here?	89
28	I Swam With The Dolphins Mum	93
29	Caroline	97
30	Jemima	101
31	Andreaus	105
32	Tim	111
33.	The Inhaler	115
34.	Advent	117
35.	A Christmas Story	119
36	Amadeus	123
37.	Amelia (?)	127

Part 2 The Poems

1	Hello Mummy	133
2	I Live A Life So Pure	134
3	I Am Here	135
4	We Come To See You	136
5	Can I Sit By Your Side	137
6	Remember	138
7	I Was Nine	139
8	There Are Lots Of Us Here	140
9	Keep A Place For Me	144
10	Hi Mummy Hi Daddy I Love You	145
11	I Wish That's How It Was	147
12	It's Getting Better	149
13	I'll Be There	150
14	Keep Me In Your Heart But Let Me Go	151

15	Forever	152
16	Has Anyone Reminded You?	153
17	How Can I Be Dead?	154
18	I Am Not Alone	155
19	Relax	156

Introduction

Several years ago two friends of mine, Peter King and his lovely wife Hilary ran a home circle, the Medium being another good friend, Mavis King (no relation whatsoever). Understandably they became known as 'The Three Kings'.

Each year they hosted a wonderful evening of Mediumship purely for children in the Spirit World to come forward and speak to their families. One year Mavis mentioned to me that she was having difficulty finding a suitable poem to read out at the Children's Evening. A phrase kept coming into my mind, so I wrote it down. Before I had finished one line another presented itself; then another; and another. Within about fifteen minutes "Hello Mummy" was written.

This was the first of many poems and pieces which arrived, and indeed continue to arrive. Most of the pieces are from children, but all from the Spirit World are welcome to share their stories. Who can explain the stories? I enjoy the English language, but the different styles and different aspects of life are beyond my understanding and capability. Nowadays I don't try to understand or explain, I just accept and am grateful.

Peter and Hilary have themselves now made their journey to the Spirit World, but Mavis continues with the work she herself does as a Medium, including helping me develop as a Medium myself: indeed as I frequently tell her, this book is 'all her fault'.

I have changed very little of what has been given to me. I am very aware that there are grammar and punctuation errors, but to correct them would have taken away the style with which the children spoke and told their tales. These are their words not mine. Take what comfort you want from the words, they have helped me over the years, I hope they at least make you think.

Karen Wood

There are many here who have stories to tell.

Listen well

Part 1
The Stories

1. *Amanda*

You're the lady I was told about. They said I could talk and you would write. Well I'm talking. I am Amanda. I am 10 and I am 'Dead poor Dear'. That's what they said. 'Dead poor Dear'. But if I'm standing here and talking to you I'm not dead am I? I am very alive. My lady says I'm very, very alive. She says my Mummy and Daddy gave me a good start because they didn't say I was going to die. They said, "Your body doesn't work but you will not have to worry about that soon, because you are going to leave it and soar up and be free and well. You will be able to sing and dance and you will be able to play again".

So when I left my body I did soar and I tried and I could dance.

I used to love dancing. I used to go to lessons as well. I used to dance all the way there and dance all the way back. My brother used to dance with me, trying to do what I did, and we used to laugh and laugh.

Then I got pains in my legs, and it didn't go away. I felt odd, and that didn't go away, like the world was tilting over on its side. I couldn't stand up, I was in bed all day and all the next day; and my neck went stiff and my head hurt, and I was very ill and I had to go to hospital. My head got better but my neck and my legs didn't, and my chest hurt too. I had to have a horrible mask to breathe through and I had to lie very still. I couldn't eat or drink by myself, but my Mummy and my Daddy were always there. They sat next to me, sometimes just Mummy and sometimes just Daddy, sometimes both of them. My brother came too - and my friends. For a while I could hear people but I couldn't see them, and I couldn't talk at all. I could waggle and wiggle with my fingers and my toes but only on one foot. My brother kept asking why I didn't wake up. But I wasn't asleep so I wiggled my fingers for him.

Then one day I felt some children come and I could see them, and they pulled my hands and I could get up and play and dance with them. They came often but in between I was lying in my bed with my mother talking to me, and telling me I would soon be able to dance without my body. I wanted to tell her I already could but I didn't know how, so I wiggled my fingers and my toes.

Then a lady came with the children, Amelia her name was, she said we were all going together this time, me, the children and her. We came here. I said, "Is this Heaven?" The lady smiled and laughed and said, "Some people think it is called Heaven. We just call it home".

2. Barry Woodentop

'Barry Woodentop'. That's what Daddy calls me, or he used to, because I used to bang my head as though it was made of wood. I don't know why I banged my head so much. It was a habit that made me feel as though the world would go away. But it didn't. It was still there when I stopped banging. Only I had a headache as well as the world. But I always had the thought that it might work.

I liked some of the world but not all of it. I liked buses, I liked ice cream; I liked swimming baths - but I didn't like swimming. We used to go and I used to sit in the water and watch while everyone else swam, but I didn't want to swim myself, so they stopped trying to make me. I liked football on TV, but I only like playing with a ball by myself not playing with others. I liked to play putting the ball in the basketball thing too, by myself. My Dad used to try and play with me but I didn't like that.

I liked school dinners; I used to sit at a table by myself. They thought they were punishing me for being naughty but I wasn't being punished; I liked sitting by myself. I didn't like it when they made me sit at a table with other people. They might have wanted my food. They kept talking to me; trying to make me join in, but I didn't like joining in and I didn't like sitting next to someone else, they were too close, so I sat by myself and I was happy then.

I liked one of my teachers, she smelled nice and she didn't stand close to me. She gave me a book to read, all about medicine and how it was invented and how people learned to use it. I liked that. I could read OK, I didn't like writing though. It was the pen - I didn't like the pen. So she gave me another pen just for me, in a case, just for me. I could put it back in the case when I had finished using it and no one else would use it. I liked that.

They were going to send me to another school without Miss Hetherington. I said I didn't want to go but they said I was too old for my school and I had to go to another one. Miss Hetherington said I could take my pen with me. But I wanted to take Miss Hetherington as well as the pen. She said she had to stay to teach the young children but that she would tell the new school all about how I liked to sit by myself and use my very own pen. But I didn't want to go.

So one day I was sitting in my bedroom watching football on TV and I decided I wasn't going to go to the new school. I would go and live at my old school all the time. There was a room under the classrooms with the boiler in it and a space at the back. I would go and live in there. So I picked up my bag from under my bed and I put in it my shoes and my socks. Four pairs of socks, and four pairs of boxers, and four shirts for school, and two pairs of trousers, and my toothbrush, and my pyjamas, and my dressing gown, and then my bag was full. But I took my bankbook. I had put all my money in so I knew I would be able to buy my tea. I would have school dinners every day.

Then I climbed out of the window and threw my bag down. But I overbalanced and fell down after my bag.

I hit my head and everything went fuzzy. Then it got brighter again and brighter still. And a lady stood there. But not too close. And she said I could stay with her in a place of my very own and not go to school.

So I came here. It's easier to think now, and I don't mind if people are near me so much. I still don't like playing football though - only by myself.

I like it here. It is peaceful and I can be alone and not have to make the world go away.

Or I can watch other people and maybe one day I will join in.

It isn't so hard now. I don't need the world to go away any more.

3. Carrie

Hi, I've been told you listen to children. Well I want to tell someone what happened to me. I was asleep and I was happy. I was dreaming about my holiday. My family were going to stay at my Grandma's house. All of us. My sister and brother, and my cousins, my aunt and uncle, all of them. I went to sleep early. I was told it would make the holiday come quicker. It didn't. I just stopped breathing. My body just stopped working. That's what they told me.

I can remember getting out of bed and I wasn't on the floor I was on the ceiling. I don't know how. For a little while I had a silvery sort of string going from me to my body, but then it wasn't there anymore and I just kept on going away from my body. I wasn't scared because I didn't know what was happening. I just kept moving. I don't know if I was walking or swimming or flying, I was just moving. It was all lovely and bright and clean and fresh and then I sort of whooshed, I don't know how. And then a lovely lady said I was a beautiful child and a lovely pureness. I didn't know what she meant so I didn't say anything.

Then I asked her if I was on holiday. It seemed a sensible question at the time. Now it seems a bit silly. But you have to do what is right at the time. And I still sort of thought I was dreaming. Someone told me I must have had someone with me but I can't remember seeing anyone, but it didn't matter because everything was just like it was right. Everything seemed natural. There wasn't any reason to be scared.

I can't remember everything that happened when I first got there. I can remember a man, well I think it was a man but that didn't matter either, saying that I was going to stay with a lovely lady. I said, "Yes, that's my Grandma". He smiled and looked gentle somehow and said this wasn't my Grandma but she was lovely all the same. I said I was going on holiday so I couldn't go and stay with her now. I had to go home now. I started getting just a bit puzzled because this wasn't like any dream I'd ever had before. I thought about other dreams and then realised that when you are dreaming you don't think about dreaming. This must be different. Then it began to dawn on me that I wasn't asleep at all. And that I wasn't in my body. Shall I tell you what my first thought was when I realised what had happened? I thought "cool". And then I thought "but I can't be dead I'm only ten". They told me that it sometimes happened like that. I mean you would have expected my Grandma to be here not me wouldn't you? It sounds bad when I tell it like this because I've never mentioned my mother or my father or any of them. But I was in a sort of cocoon if you can understand that. I was just going along with whatever they said and whatever I felt. I didn't fight anything because everything felt right, everything felt fine. So I just went along with it.

That's what I wanted to tell you. That it isn't scary dying, that you don't have to worry, and that you parents who have seen your children come over here don't have to be sorry about them. It's set up really well.

Children are very important. No, that's not the right word. They are very precious. They are looked after really well. They have fun - but in that fun they learn lots and lots. They see lots and lots about everything, whatever they need to learn about. It isn't like school. We don't get homework. They just let us learn what we want to learn or what we need to learn. I don't have to learn some things. I already know about emotions and crying so I don't need to learn them. I had a happy life. I'm having a happy new life.

It's my other birthday soon. We have two. One when we were born as a baby. One when we come here. Everything is cool. I'm happy.

Tell everyone for me please?

Carrie

4 Alicia

Come on over here said the man – well I wasn't going to fall for that one – so I ran the other way. There were lots of people nearby and my Daddy always said if I'm in trouble run to a crowd. Bad people don't like drawing attention to themselves – so I ran towards the crowd. It would have worked but I ran over a road and got knocked down by a car. Silly wasn't I? But Stella says better than not running away.

I'm happy – it's all kind of bubbly here. I have lots and lots of friends and I can be whoever and whatever I want to be. I wasn't a big girl - so I am going to be tall. I wasn't a naughty girl - but I'm not going to be naughty now. I'm just going to have fun because you can learn a lot having fun. I can sing and dance and laugh and run and play games and see the animals. I love that; going to see the animals. I can slide on the giraffes' necks and ask a snake if I can use him as a rope to skip with. We always ask first. It would be wrong not to. And I love playing with the cats. Not the dogs, but I may want to another time. I didn't like dogs you see. My friend had a really big dog and it used to bark very loudly and I didn't like that. So I don't see the dogs much. But they can't bite me here so one day I might go to see them, but not yet.

I go to see my Mummy a lot. She is recovering from her loss. I go to see Daddy too. Mummy and Daddy have decided to try living apart for a little while to see if they can be better friends. I go to see both of them and they are both doing very well. Daddy thought Mummy should have been with me the day I got run over, but he tried very, very hard not to say that to her. She knew he thought it though. She thought the same thing but she was busy and I had gone to the shops with my friend. She had just gone down the road to her house, and I was going down the other road to mine, when the man shouted over to me and I ran back towards the shops. It wasn't Mummy's fault was it? I forgot to look at the road. But I'm happy.

I miss my cat and my rabbit and I miss Mummy and Daddy. But I want Mummy and Daddy to be a proper Mummy and Daddy together again. I want them to live in the same house again. Daddy misses Mummy. Mummy is missing Daddy but not quite ready to tell him so yet. She will one day I hope.

Can you put down that all the Mummies and Daddies should be very very nice to each other because it makes a tremendous different to how we settle down in our new world? Thank you for letting me come and see you.

Alicia (?)

5 On The Train

Covering all contingencies I should have been able to be home for Christmas, but I hadn't of course covered the most important contingency. I didn't allow for the fact that the man sitting next to me on the train had a belt full of dynamite and that he would at a point in the journey blow himself and a carriage full of strangers straight into the next world.

I had no chance to escape as I was trapped next to the window and I went the same instant he did. I saw him as he emerged into this new world of ours. Funny you think there is only one white tunnel but what there seemed to be that day was one for each of us – our own personal white light.

He was jubilant that he had done his God's work. He seemed to be seeing a different new world from me. He was seeing glory and happiness and I was seeing life without my family, and without my friends. I was in shock I know that, but I needed to confront him – I needed to say to him, "Why?" But when I spoke to him – shouted to him even – it was as though I didn't exist. He was on a high enjoying the delights of his new life he seemed sure were waiting for him.

The man who was helping me said he would see life as he expected it for a while but slowly it would dawn on him that perhaps, just possibly, it was not the same paradise as he expected and that his 'martyrdom' was not giving him a higher position than the white men and the 'oppressors' he had taken with him. He was not an evil man. He was confused, possibly unbalanced, certainly completely convinced that he was in the right, but not evil. The evil ones were the people who convinced him to take his actions. They were the ones who would have to face their victims one day. The man who sent me here was deluded what more can I say? Blaming him, cursing him, wanting to fight him, shake sense into him – all this went through my mind for a while but to what purpose? Eventually I learned to accept what had happened.

I learned that my family, though still in shock, would be cared for, counselled, helped financially and supported, but whatever happened I could not go back. I had this crazy idea for a while that I could be like one of the characters in those films and videos who got a second chance and went back for a while to sort out their affairs. But of course that is only a film not real life. And the reality was that I had died. A healthy fit young man on his way home to his family to enjoy a well-earned break was dead. Gone. Forever. Well gone from my family's point of view anyway.

I had had no preconceived idea of what happened when you 'died', 'passed on', 'expired', 'deceased', whatever name you want to put on it. So I suppose it took me less time than some to adjust to having no body. The body I had always looked after in the belief that it would then look after me in the later stages of my life. But of course I HAD no later stages.

I left my body in a million pieces in the wreckage of the train. There was nothing for my family to bury, only a twisted piece of metal that was identified as possibly being part of a bracelet I had been wearing. Not much to put in a coffin was it? My family did not have that 'closure' I suppose some would call it.

And here I was. Would you like me to describe this place as I see it? Well it would be difficult to let you know exactly what I am experiencing because you have not the experience of the colours and the brightness that I have all around me. Not brightness that is harsh, just so much clearer than anything on earth. I asked if it was the lack of pollution that made everything so great, but they said the human eye is not capable of seeing the clarity and that it would not seem so even if they had the chance. We would see what our eyes could take. So I cannot explain exactly what I see, but I can say that there is nothing harsh to see, everything is clear, and somehow seems right. The sounds are clearer too; again, your ears do not have the capability of hearing the sounds as clearly as we do. But to us, well it is harmonious; I suppose that is the best word. Sweet I suppose but not a word I would normally use.

Experiences again are difficult to explain. If I want anything, I have it. Sounds wonderful doesn't it, and I suppose it is in a way, but it is not the same as having something that you have worked and earned the money for. It doesn't have that same satisfaction, but the satisfaction is still there, merely different. I am still learning new experiences every day; every hour if you like but we do not have clocks so I am not able to measure time in that way.

We never feel cold, or hungry, or unwell, in fact the opposite is true. We feel so well we could almost burst with it.

So I am living a life, and it is a life believe me, that is warm, safe, colourful, with wonderful sounds, wonderful experiences and good people around me who answer all my never ending questions with patience and humour. And I ask many questions, as anyone who knew me in my time with a body would testify, that has not changed.

Would I come back now if I had the chance? To be with my family possibly, to take up my old life, no certainly not. I have found what I thought I never would. I have found that life can be calm and satisfying. And I feel good.

6 Flat On Fire!

My brother and I decided it would be a bit of a laugh to set fire to the house and call the brigade out. If you are going to do that you need to get out fast. You need to work out first that the door isn't locked or at least have a key in it. We didn't. So we couldn't get out. We broke the window but there was nowhere to jump to and it just fanned the flames higher. We were stuck in there.

Another thing you need to know is that there isn't a big fire in the town that night, so the brigade can't get to small ones so fast. So there we were - flat on fire – stuck in there and no fire brigade.

The smoke alarm was working but mum often burned food so no one took any notice when it went off. That didn't help us any. In the end my brother jumped out of the window out of sheer fright. I was coughing by that time and couldn't see properly.

I heard a screech of brakes and realised my brother had hit the pavement. He lived – after a fashion – for a while. My mother came back from work late that night by which time I was well gone – and so was the flat.

Its funny you know I was a bit scared when I got here. I thought I was going to be in big trouble cos I was the eldest so it was really my fault more than his. But no one told me off at all. But I did have to see the effect it had on my mother. And my Dad when he found out.

He didn't live with us so he only found out when a mate at work told him. My mother said he never bothered with us while we were alive so why bother him now. That was what hurt him most at first – that he wasn't told. Not that we had died – just that he wasn't told.

He wanted to know if there was an insurance claim but there wasn't a pay out because they realised we had lit the fire ourselves and also that we were in the flat on our own and we shouldn't have been. Big deal. We had spent every night on our own since Dad left while Mum worked.

She wasn't a bad mother just so tired and run down all the time. She worked at the club on a night. It was all she could get. So she was home when we came home from school and she fed us OK but then she had to go to work and we had to get ourselves to bed. I was supposed to make sure we went to bed at the right time but I never did. The neighbours used to 'tut-tut' at her and complain at us. But they should have tried it from our side. If they were that concerned why didn't they help us? Why didn't they come sit with us? We would have liked that – we got scared sometimes on our own if it was thundering or lightning; and we couldn't go out on Halloween or anything like that.

It was near bonfire night it happened. We were pretending to be burglars and then we were Guy Fawkes and his men – and then we decided if we set fire to the flat we could be little heroes and save each other. So we set off some paper in an ashtray – It got hold really well. The idea was for me to call the brigade while my brother dashed for help – but the brigade didn't come and the door was locked – without a key. And that was that really. I woke up here.

My mother is now having some help to get over it – and my Dad? Well he is drinking – and using us as an excuse so that people feel sorry for him. But most people see through him. It was his drinking was the start of it really, I know that now. He drank the money for food – Mum cried – he hit out - she threw him out – so we were on our own. End of story.

But it isn't the end – it's our beginning. 10 years old I was. Now I'm 12 I think.

By for now

Mark (or Marcus)

7 Goodness Gracious

Goodness Gracious Gollydrops Gumboots. That what my Granddad used to say to me if I made him jump. He was funny my Granddad. We used to laugh a lot and he used to tickle me so I laughed more. And then one day he ran me over.

He didn't mean to. His car didn't turn the way it was supposed to. My Granddad was questioned by the Policeman but my Mummy and Daddy said he would never hurt a hair on my head intentionally. The Policeman checked the car and it was faulty and they let Granddad go home. He wasn't relieved, he was just upset and devastated because he said what did it matter if he was guilty or innocent; he could never forgive himself for my death.

My Daddy was too upset to talk to him much because he was supposed to have checked the car for him and he forgot. So he thought it was his fault, but Mummy said it wasn't because that wasn't why he was checking the car. It wasn't anybody's fault it just happened. I got a shock and a Golly Gosh Gumdrops fright and then I ended up here. I can't remember coming here. I just remember seeing the car come right up to me and then I was here and a man was telling me to relax because I wasn't hurting so I didn't have to be frightened. I said I wasn't frightened I was just Goodness Gracious Gollydrops Gumboots shocked and he laughed.

I went to where there were lots of children playing. They all sat together and held hands and held my hands and said hello to me. I've got a new best friend now called Jake. He's funny. He never lived on earth. He says bodies are silly and its better not to have one. He says what do we need them for? He's always managed *'per-fect-ly'* well without one and he is *'per-fect-ly'* happy without living on our earth.

I told him we liked having bodies because we could eat ice cream and chips and go swimming and get cold and then have warm drinks and cuddly hugs. So we have decided its good both ways. Stella said we are sensible boys to work it out. She says we are very clever young men. She is pretty. We like her. We really do.

When we get older we will do some work but I don't know what to do yet. Stella says I can think about it when I am ready. Jake is thinking about it now but he keeps changing his mind. Stella says this is quite right. He should cover every possibility first.

My Granddad is in my world now. They say he had a heart attack brought on by grief, so they let me go and see him when he was ready. I took Jake with me so we could show Granddad how good we were together as friends. Stella said Granddad was much helped by our visit. We will go and see him again one day.

8 A Night Out With Friends

Hi I'm here. I want to tell you what is going on in my life right now. Well it's my death so far as you are concerned. Death – funny word – what does it mean? Look it up. It probably says an ending. But an ending of what? Not of me. I'm more me than ever. I'm just more. More vibrant, more alive, bright, more energy – more everything.

I was out for the evening with friends when it happened. We were all in a pub – trying to pretend we were old enough to be there you know? Well two out of the five of us were. So we thought if they went and bought the drinks we were OK. And we were drinking out of bottles so that no one could spike our drinks. Well that was the idea. Of course what I didn't take into account was that the drink was spiked by my friend. So when it arrived at the table the damage was already done.

I just thought I was getting drunk very quickly; everything was spinning. Not just the room – me as well. It was as though I was spinning one way and the room spinning the other way. At first it was funny. But then I couldn't talk properly and my friends were laughing at me. Then their faces changed and they started shouting at me. I knew I was being shouted at but what they were saying didn't make sense to me and I couldn't answer them. And I couldn't stand up or walk at all. Then everything kept fading in and out.

I remember a policeman – at least I think it was a policeman – a man with a uniform anyway – he kept trying to talk to me but I couldn't understand him either. Then I suppose I was in an ambulance and my legs and my arms - all of me really – was twitching on its own. Someone put something over my face – I think it was a mask or something – but I think I vomited.

Then it all went dark – and then sort of light and dark together and a man and a lady – the lady looking sort of sad and saying, "It's all right dear you are safe"; and the man saying, "Stay calm son – it's OK." I didn't know who they were – I hadn't seen them before. I thought they must be Doctors or Nurses of some kind. I said, "Where am I – who are you?" You know; the daft questions you ask when you wake from a really deep sleep? Only I wasn't waking up I was dying.

I wish I could say I saw my body and people working on it but I didn't – I suppose I just didn't think to look. Anyway the lady said would I like to come with her because there was no use in hanging around here. Funny you know – your parents spend years in telling you not to talk to strangers - but these two, the man and the lady, didn't seem at all strange - it seemed totally OK to go with them, so I did. I went along with them.

I don't remember much except that we got brighter and brighter. I don't mean I went into a tunnel of light; we might have but I didn't notice. I just got brighter and brighter and then saw my Granddad. I thought that was cool, I loved my Granddad. He had died two years before me and I missed him. He said, "Well you were a prat weren't you? Never mind it can't be helped".

The woman who was standing next to him looked a little shocked as though he shouldn't have said that. But that's how he always reacted if I'd done something daft. So if he hadn't said that I wouldn't have felt so safe. And I did feel safe somehow. I sort of knew I had died but it hadn't really sunk in then you know. Anyhow I stayed with Granddad; or rather he stayed with me for a while.

I got a bit frightened at one time but a lady who was sort of sparkly somehow said "Go in there for a while you will feel better." I went into what I suppose was a sort of bubbly thing. It was *wow* all sort of safe and floaty and I felt sleepy and nothing mattered anymore, and I stayed there till I felt like coming out again.

Anyway I'm here and I'm OK. I sort of miss being down there with my mates and having a laugh but its OK here. There are other kids like me and I've been spending time with them and a man who sort of has the answers to any question I ever think of. And my Granddad of course. He's here whenever I think about him. I don't even have to ask for him – I think of him and he's here. Granddad says when I'm ready he will let me go back to see my Mum and Dad, but not yet.

My Mum is having a hard time of it. She thought I was doing my college work at a mate's house. The Police had to tell her I had been in a pub, had taken something and had a bad reaction and had died on the way to hospital. She blames herself. She says she had a feeling I was lying to her but wanted to trust me, so she didn't stop me going. Now she says if only she had. But it was an accident waiting to happen.

We had all been laughing for weeks about going for a drink. Sixteen we were, all out of school and at college. Only 6th form but it said college. Men of the world we thought we were. Adults.

And of course two of my mates were eighteen; one of them just two days before so we went with them. One of them was a bit of a loony; used to try selling pills and things his brother had got for him. He didn't take them himself just sold them for money. He used to buy DVD's and stuff with the money. He wasn't a dealer or anything – well I didn't think so anyway. But he thought it would be a giggle to put one in my drink.

He isn't laughing now. He's been charged; and his brother; and his brother's mate who got the stuff. So they tell me anyway. I've not been back to see. What's the point? It's happened. It's done. I'm here – I'm OK. That's what I wanted to say. If anyone hears this or reads it – let them know what a joke can do. It's messed up my life, my mother's and father's, my kid brother's, my mate, his brother and his mate, their parents, and the kids at school and college. Not so funny now is it?

9 How Are You Doing World?

When I first came over here I wasn't sure what to expect. I was told about Heaven by an old Priest in my little town north of West Virginia. If you were good you went to Heaven. If you weren't – well you would wish you had been. Talk about Hell, fire and brimstone. Anyway here I am.

Falling off a bus while playing about with my friends just about gave me a sure-fire ticket. I 'woke up' with all these smiling faces around me. They weren't anyone I knew. Well I didn't know many of my family much. My father was 'no good' my mother wasn't much better; I ran away when I was twelve. I existed off my wits for a few years and then there was the bus. It seemed a good idea at the time. Hang on to the back of a bus and go for a free ride. Except my hands slipped and I went straight under the wheels of a truck following behind.

Anyway like I said I woke up with all these strange faces smiling at me. That was a novelty; people usually told me to "Get out of it you little varmint" (or words like that anyway). They told me I had come home. Well I wasn't having that - what was the point of running away if they were going to take me back.

Then one of them explained that it wasn't my earthly home but my final home. I could rest and let other people take over now at least for a while, till I felt stronger sort of thing. I was a bit suspicious. Then they let me go to sleep – which was strange 'cos I didn't feel tired at all and then I just sort of drifted off. I was aware of things around me but I couldn't talk to anyone – I didn't have the energy and anyway it was nice and quiet – not like the streets where I had been living.

And I felt lovely and clean and free and just like I remember when I went to stay with some family or other when I was a little un (when my mother was drunk I expect). The sheets were all nice and clean and sweet smelling and warm and safe somehow. Anyway that's the sort of feeling I got when I was drifting.

Then I started slowly to see things from my life. It was strange. I knew it was me, but it didn't feel like me. I was just sort of observing. I saw me being hit by my Dad. I saw me in a dirty nappy when my Mum was asleep and I saw me crying 'cos I was hungry. Then I saw me pulling a fly apart and crying. All sorts of things. I also saw the Priest giving me a bag of food to take to my Mum. I guess he wasn't all wrong. Oh there was lots of things going on. But I was somehow detached from it all – like I said.

After I had seen all of that and had a talk with some women and a man in a gold coat I was given someone to show me around. This man had been through a lot the same as me, but he had come over much later on in life than me. He was 43 when he was killed in a fight. He had managed on his own from about 8 'cos his mother was killed by his father and he ran away before it happened to him as well. He seemed to have all the time in the world to take me wherever I wanted to go and do whatever I wanted to do. I asked him why he bothered with me and didn't he have anything better to do. Once I asked if he didn't trust me 'cos I could never get away from him. I tried too. He said he would leave me when I was ready to be left. It dawned on me that I would have been frightened if I was on my own.

It seemed such a big place, and sometimes it seemed to be all sorts of different places all rolled into one. I asked him what people did for fun and he said whatever they wanted to do. I said I wanted to go and have a drink. He laughed and took me to somewhere that was just like the places back home. A man handed me a drink. I took it and then realised that this was crazy. You can't drink if you are dead. He laughed again – and said if you wanted to imagine you are drinking then you can be. And all these people wanted to imagine they were. I stayed for a while, but you don't get drunk on that sort of drinking so what's the use? I wandered around for a while – the old man just sort of tagged along – and then I went where I had been when I woke up.

They said I didn't need to be with them anymore, but I could stay for a while if I wanted to. I said I didn't know where else to go and they told me the old man had found me somewhere. They actually had houses for people to stay in. They looked like brick ones to me but I guess they can't really have been. I mean how could they mix the base? Anywhere there I was sleeping in a house again, the first time for years. There were other people there but they didn't bother me too much. I liked one feeling a lot – or rather a lack of feeling – I didn't feel hungry any more. Can't remember the last time that happened.

The old man – Harry his name was – introduced me to some other kids he said I might like to spend time with. There was one who was called Butch and another called Sam. They were OK really, and I kind of started feeling a bit more at home. I asked them who ran things around here. They said everyone ran things for themselves. This didn't seem right to me. I mean where I came from any new kid had to prove himself if he wanted to stay in one piece. Butch laughed at that and said "How they going to take you apart here then? You're already dead!" I couldn't get round that one for a while. Then he told me that there was no need to fight each other here because there was nothing to grab possession of. If you wanted anything you only had to think of it and it was there. But he told me you soon got sick of wanting great big bikes and cars and stereos and that 'cos there was no need for cars and such – if you wanted to go anywhere you just had to think of it and you were there. And if you wanted music you heard it just like that.

It was my idea of Heaven then for a while. I rode bikes and raced cars with myself and listened to music, and then it dawned on me that I could see and feel the bikes and cars, and hear the music, but no one else could unless they wanted to, and that wasn't much fun after a while.

Then the old man was there again and he asked me if I would like to go back to the 'Earth Plains' again and I said, "OK why not?" But it isn't as easy as I thought; the first time I tried I pulled back. It was a really weird experience, all sort of squiggly and strange. I felt kind of nauseous which was funny because I didn't have anything to upchuck or to upchuck with. I didn't try it again for ages. I don't know how long 'cos there are no clocks here. Then I did manage it and everything felt really, really strange and kind of dull. Everything looked sort of grey and cloudy and not as solid as where we have been.

I saw the old gang again and I kind of felt sad for a while, but when the old man asked me if I would like to be back with them I realised that I had sort of got used to where I was now living. So we went back. Kind of sneaky really wasn't it? Just when I was getting bored with things he goes and shows me how REALLY boring life had been when I was "down there".

So now I'm getting on with things, and maybe I will hang around with Butch and Sam and another guy I just met called Smoky for a while until I decide what I want to do next. Because that's what happens here. You do one thing until you want to do something else. And then they find something else for you to do. If I want to I can work. Not keen on that for an idea but Butch says he probably will soon. So who knows maybe sometime? Anyway that's all for now. Just wanted to tell you about me. See ya.

(BART? OR BARTHOLOMEW?)

10 I Didn't Wake Up

I didn't wake up. I was asleep and I didn't wake up. My mum called and called and my brother shook me but I didn't wake up. I wasn't dead I just didn't wake up. My Mummy called the ambulance and the man and lady came in to my bedroom and tried to wake me up, but I didn't wake up. I never woke up again.

I don't know how long I was like that. I just know I was here and I'm wide, wide awake.

It's sunny but it's not too hot so we can play without having to put cream on. We don't get hungry so we don't have to eat. I didn't like eating. If we are busy we can carry right on without stopping. We don't get tired. We don't have to sleep and we still don't have to eat or drink – so if we are learning something we can keep on learning till we finish learning. So it's easier than on earth.

We do have a change now and then because it makes it interesting. And we learn as much as we want to and then we can keep on learning for as long as we want to. We don't have to stop because school has finished; and we have no homework.

They say I had wasted away because I didn't eat. My Mummy tried to make me eat. She really did. She tried to make me drink drinks with food in them – nourishment – but I wouldn't drink them. I wasn't trying to be thin. I just didn't like eating. So I didn't eat.

I miss being with my cat but I don't mind not being with my family too much because I still am with them in a way. I go to see them a lot and my brother can see me and hear me so I can still talk to him. He says he likes eating so he isn't coming over here. He sometimes used to eat my food for me if we were both given our meal and I didn't want to eat mine. But he wasn't being greedy, he just didn't like to see Mummy and I getting cross with each other because she wanted me to eat and I didn't want to. So when Mummy left the room I would put my food in his plate and he would eat it. Then Mummy would let us get down from the table. He is younger than me but now he says he is going to be older because he is going to have a birthday and be 9. He is funny.

Don't be cross with my brother. He is my best friend and he didn't know I would die if I didn't eat. And, I don't mind being dead because I don't have to eat anymore. I didn't like the thought of all that food sitting in my stomach and going off in there. They said it was a phobia. My Granny said, "Let her go hungry she will eat when she is ready". But I didn't, and then I didn't wake up. My bed was all comfy and I was tired so I didn't get up some days. My teeth were all wobbly and my skin went funny. But I didn't believe it was because I didn't eat. I just got more and more tired so I stayed in bed.

And then I didn't wake up. It's OK being dead. I'm happier now than I was. Please don't be upset for me. I wouldn't ever have got used to eating. I've seen some people be taken into hospital and be put on machines that push food into them or have tubes into their stomachs for the food to go in. I wouldn't have liked that. It was the food in my stomach I didn't want. So now I don't have a stomach and I'm happy. Be happy for me will you?

They say I don't have to give you my name unless I want to. But if I give you my name people will say my Mummy should have known better. But it wasn't her fault. She didn't know how good I was at not eating or drinking. I would drink water but not stuff with food in. I used to put it in the loo, or in the plant, or give it to the cat, or my brother, or out of the window, or in my bag, or under cushions, or anywhere. But not eat it.

I have to go now. We are going to go out and see some mountains and walk right up to the top and look at the people climbing them who will be struggling. But we won't, we can run up if we like.

I'm happy here. Don't be sad for me. And don't be cross with Mummy. She did her best. She just didn't know why I didn't want to eat. I just didn't know why everyone else wanted to eat. So that's that. Goodbye.

11 I Fought In The War

I heard you talking about the war and I had to tell you what happened to me. I was 17 when I left home. It all seemed glorious then, going off to war in your bright red uniform. The ladies blowing us kisses, the gentlemen raising their hats to us. It felt just grand.

Then we set off. The train carriages were a bit bleak. Standing for most of the way. I think they had been used for cattle; they had a very strange smell to them. The train was noisy too and very dirty. Most of us had dirt on our uniforms by the time we got off. The officers yelled and cursed us. We couldn't do much about it. There was nowhere for us to clean up. The officers had people to help them, and they weren't in the same carriages as us. They were in comfortable seats with tables and stuff like that, and mirrors on the wall.

We went to the docks and got on board a ship. Have you ever felt seasick? I was ill all the way, and I wasn't near the rails of the ship. We were very crowded. Again the officers were inside in the warm and dry being served drinks. I had never seen the sea before let alone sailed on it. I wanted to go home and forget all the ideas of grandeur that had been fed to us.

This wasn't glamorous and it wasn't exiting. It was cold, wet, miserable and frightening. I wanted my Mum to take it all away. I dreamed of being by the fire at home with Mum serving me hot soup, home-made from vegetables grown in our garden, and chicken bones from the bird we had killed the day before. I don't know how long we were on the ship but it seemed like forever.

When we arrived we were herded like cattle into troops. We had had no proper training apart from a few weeks before we set off being shown how to march round a square and how to carry a rifle. There weren't any squares to march round and we didn't all have rifles yet. If the enemy had attacked we couldn't have done anything about it. I remember lots of mud and rocks and wet slippery grass. And the cold; I had been cold since we set off. The rain never seemed to stop either. I couldn't remember the last time I had been dry or warm or comfortable. We fed all right but not in the warm or dry. Sometimes we had Messes to eat out of but usually we just sat around outside. But always the Officers were made comfortable. That was beginning to be an obsession with me. They were always so much better looked after. As my mate said who was going to do the work anyway when we got to the other end? The Officers weren't going to be the first ones in the firing line. So why were we suffering so much and they were laughing and joking and being so warm and dry and eating so much better than us.

Anyway when the action started I was in a trench with a mate and some other men, well boys really, we were all about the same age. The Sergeant with us was older, and a bit worn down by life. It was as though he'd seen it all before. You could tell he didn't expect any of us to get out alive.

Then all hell broke loose. Noise and smells and sights you couldn't describe. The man next to me got his face blown off. His blood was all over my jacket. My jacket, which had been so gloriously red and bright when I set off. Now it was filthy dirty and torn. And now covered in blood. That showed darker. And the smell of it. One other problem. You can't just nip off to the little boy's room in the middle of all that. And seeing your mate killed -you can imagine the rest.

I can't tell you whether or not I killed anyone. I just fired and fired and fired. We didn't get out of that trench for what seemed like days. Only two of us got out. Me and the Sergeant. I could tell you lots of what went on in there. But I don't like remembering it all. Just as we got out and started running back along the lines an Officer saw us and ordered us into another trench. The Sergeant turned round and set off towards the other trench.

I suddenly saw myself as I had been. Young, bright, not too bad looking, the world at my feet. I had escaped being killed for days on end. Very little food. Horrible water to drink. Seeing friends and strangers killed all round me. Not really knowing why we were fighting. No one giving me any respect. No one explaining anything properly. The all the noise and sights and smells of war. The fear deep in your stomach. You don't act from bravery or cowardice at a time like that. You act from fright. Then this pig of an Officer telling me to go and do it again. I couldn't. I just couldn't. So I ran.

I don't know where I was running to I was just running. Away. Anywhere other than back to that stinking war. I felt a searing pain in my back. Then another. And another. And I woke up here. It took a long time to adjust to being dead. It took a long time before I accepted that I was dead. I kept on running.

I was too scared to listen to the man who tried to help me. I just ran and ran and ran. It finally dawned on me that no matter how hard I ran this man was always there when I looked round.

He wasn't out of breath either. It didn't dawn on me at first that neither was I. When he finally told me that my war was over I cried. Not from joy or even relief – I just cried. It had all been so horrible. A nightmare.

They told my mother I was a coward. She never got over it. She didn't believe it but she couldn't cope with other people telling her it. The man who shot me got his the same day. I've seen him a few times since. He and I have had a lot of talks. He now knows why I ran. I now know why he had to shoot. I won't say we are friends; but I don't hate him any more.

But I can't see the point of war. I have watched wars from over here. It's strange. Some armies treat their men better now than we were. Others are just as bad or even worse. Even now. No one ever really understands what is going on.

You have a remembrance time when you think of all the men who died for you. Please don't let anyone tell you we did it for the next generations. We did it for ourselves. We set off for the glory and excitement. We had this high ideal that we were brainwashed with. But in the end we did it for ourselves. I did anyway.

12 I Never Lived On Your Earth

I never lived on your earth, but you see that means I don't have any worries about leaving people behind. I go to see the family that would have been mine and I do love them dearly, but I don't have the strong bonds that those children who lived their short lives with their parents seem to have formed.

I do not miss that because you can't miss what you have never had. I can only say I have a very happy life and I had a very happy childhood. Does that seem strange to you? That I had a childhood at all? I have heard that it is thought that we appear in the Spirit World as some kind of Angel or perhaps a Cherub.

The egg that would have been a baby was brought to the Spirit World. If you want to know how that happens it takes someone cleverer than me to describe it but I can only say that I know it happens. I suppose you must call it a kind of incubation area where all the babies live until they are ready to be born. Not their bodies but their spirits are born. Not a sudden birth as on earth, I think I am glad I did not have to do that. But a gradual time of a baby mind developing. That is what comes to us – the mind. Of course the mind is not a fully formed rational thinking mind with full knowledge; that would not be sensible.

So this pure tiny mind needs first of all to know love and safe feeling, and that it has been given as it matured as an egg.

There are special areas that are given to the nurturing of that tiny precious mind, and that is where I went after my incubation stage. To a place where tiny seeds of minds are allowed to begin the process of growing into mature minds capable of so, so much. Here we learn to recognise sights and sounds and smiles, just as a small baby would on earth, and at something similar to the same time scale.

At about 2 years old the baby spirit joins the group to which he or she will form bonds which will last for a very long time. These are sometimes called family groups and will sometimes have members of the same family in them. So if your brother or sister has also come to our world, then the chances are you will grow in the same group. There can be any number of us in these groups and we have some lovely older spirits who help to look after us. They teach us to laugh and love and learn, oh and also to experience the more unpleasant emotions that beset those of you who live on earth. We don't stay with them but we learn what it feels like to be afraid, to be angry, and to be bewildered. Well I am often bewildered so I must have learned that one very well.

We also explore your world to see what makes the people of your world be as they are. We visit those of our family who still live on earth and we get to know those of our families who live now in the world we inhabit. So I got to know my grandfather, and my grandmother, and my sister and my brother and my aunts and uncles and, oh lots of relatives. I have learned so much from them. They have such wonderful knowledge, and also such a sense of humour. That is something we learn very quickly, how to laugh. Because if you can keep laughing then you can keep happy. And we are very happy.

We do learn to be curious, and this stays with us. If you are not curious you will not learn, because you will not want to experience new knowledge; new intelligences if you like.

I am enjoying my life, and I love coming to see you in your world. I am older myself now, and am learning to help others who come to our world before those of you in yours think it would be time. But what is time? We don't worry about time. We do what has to be done when it has to be done. If it takes one hundred years then it takes that time. If it takes five seconds then that is the time it takes. We don't have to stop to go to sleep, or go visit the bathroom, or to eat. We can concentrate on what we are doing and carry on until we are finished. Or the time is right for us to move on.

I cannot say whether I would have been happier on your earth as a child, but I suspect that if I had been born into my body, then I may have not had the freedom of movement that many children have. I also suspect that my brain may not have functioned as it should. These events happen. But they did not happen to me, because my mother's body did not keep my spirit inside it. So we will never know will we? But I am happy. What more can anyone want?

Be confident in the knowledge that those children who grow in Spirit grow strong in mind and strong in knowledge, and most importantly of all, they grow strong in love.

Thank you for letting me talk to you.

13 I Travelled With My Mother

I travelled with my mother. We went all over the place; Paris, New York, Frankfurt, Switzerland, Sweden. Then I got ill and we had to stay in Berlin. I didn't like the hospital it had a funny smell but Mummy said it was frightfully clean so I stayed there. I didn't get better. I stayed there till I died. That is what they called it but I haven't died. I'm here am I not?

My Mummy let them use bits of me to help other children. I go to see them. It's funny. There is a little girl who sees through my eyes and a little boy who has my lungs. I thought it was funny seeing them running around because I died. Serena said it was worthwhile. She says good came to their families because sadness had come to mine. It helped my Mummy she said.

I go to see my Mummy. She has 'come to terms with her loss' she tells people. But in her mind in the middle of the night she wonders if it was her fault. She wonders if I wouldn't have been ill if we had stayed in one place. But one place wasn't enough. I learned a lot of different languages and I knew where a lot of places were. And I learned history from reading about things in museums and listening to guides when we walked round places and I had lots of books to read; thin ones like guidebooks so we could travel with them. I never went to school because we were always travelling from place to place. Mummy said the universe was the best school of all.

I had a Daddy, but he wasn't suitable so Mummy left him behind. She said we were better on our own. I always had somewhere to sleep but sometimes it wasn't as good as it might have been. Mummy said 'it was enlightening'. Sometimes it was very good and Mummy said it was 'a marvelous opportunity'. I have often wondered what would have happened if I had gone to school and we had stayed in one place.

We were happy, and if we got bored or stopped being happy – well we travelled. Mummy didn't like to be tied down but she said I was her saving grace. She said I enriched her life. She was the one constant thing in my life I suppose. I worried about her after I left her. But Serena said I would be able to help her by giving her mental hugs and by letting her know I loved her by reminding her of the little things; like whenever we passed where there were daffodils I would pick her one because everyone can spare one daffodil. And if we were where there were pretty shells I would find her the prettiest one on the beach, and she would change it for the last prettiest one from the last place. So we didn't take anything from the sea, we just moved it around a little.

I still travel now but sometimes I like to stay still and let things happen. Mummy travels now but she doesn't sleep in beds so often now. She just stops walking and finds shelter. She carries her bag with her now too. We used to send them on ahead sometimes, but Mummy never does that now. She travels light. She says she has freedom, but Serena says it's because she can travel faster because she is escaping. Serena says she will stop running one day and be happy with herself. I hope so. If you see her will you tell her I love her please? And love her yourself too, because I don't think she is very good at loving herself. Thank you

Lorilee (Laura Lee?) 4th Oct 2004

14 Counting

I used to count all the squares on the pavement, and all the tiles in the bathroom, and all the lampposts we passed in the car. And how many footsteps it took to get to somewhere. A – B Daddy called it. I liked counting. I didn't like reading or writing but I liked counting. I used to count the grapes on the bunch, and the matches in the box beside the candle. I used to count the stars in the sky. I used to drive Daddy quite upset. But I liked counting. So I counted.

I used to have to go to see a sort of Doctor because I didn't do very well at school. He was suggesting I went to a different school. He said he knew one that looked after boys who liked to count but not to read and write. So I did not mind going there. Mummy said "No, No, No he isn't going to go to a special school. He is a bright boy they just aren't bringing it out of him". I was a bit surprised at that, because I didn't see how they could bring it out of me to read and write if I didn't want to.

Anyway I was in hospital sometimes because I had a hole in my heart and I was going to have an operation to sew it up. But when I went to sleep I woke up here. And I don't have to try to read and write ever again. But I can still count. So I do.

15 Keep Your Head Down

Keep your head down – look at your books. Don't go out to play till you have finished your work. Don't leave the table till you've finished your food. Don't go to bed till you've finished your work. Clear the table. Wash the pots. Scrub the floor. Doesn't matter if you cough. Doesn't matter if you are ill or if you are hungry. Get back to work.

Your friends call - you can't go out, the floor is dirty. Your teacher says your work is skimped, that you fall asleep. She says "Don't let her play till her work is done". She doesn't know I'm tired **because** I can't go to bed till my work is done. I can't start my work till I've finished my meal. I can't start my meal till I've finished my homework. So I rush through my homework. I don't have time. My meal is poor. It tastes bad. I have to force it down. I hate it here.

My mother sent me to stay here to get an education. But my education is suffering because of the work. My family are so proud because I am over here and going to school. They don't know about the work. They just think my aunt gets me to help around the house a little. Which I would do. But I do all the housework, and it's hard. And I have to prepare their food. It's not the same as I get. Or rather got, I'm not there now am I? Sometimes I think I'm still there. I'm told that will pass. That I will learn to be happy and that I will relax a little. I just feel I have let my parents down. I couldn't take it any more. One day I threw down my brush and said, "I'm going to bed I'm too tired". My uncle beat me. He hit me on my head and I fell down the stairs. I don't think my parents know yet. I should have worked harder, but I was too tired.

My parents don't know what happened yet.

17th and 18th October 2004

16 Miranda

My name is Miranda and I am eight years old. I died. Well they say I died but I can't have if I'm here can I? I was not ill for very long. I caught a cold and I had to stay in bed. I heard my Mum say, "It's gone to her chest". The Doctor gave me some medicine to take. It didn't taste nice.

Then I got worse, and worse, and worse. It was the medicine. My body didn't like it. And I came here. I was asleep and Tommy and the others came to see me. Tommy sat on my chest and said, "You can come with us". I said, "Get off my chest I'm poorly". He said I wasn't going to be poorly any more and I could come and swim with them. I said, "I can't swim" and he said, "Yes you can now".

I woke up and my chest and my tummy hurt. So I went back to sleep because they didn't hurt when I was asleep. Tommy was there again, and Sylvia. She was older than Tommy but she laughed as much as him. She said they were going to stay with me until I got out of my body. I said I didn't want to get out of my body and she said, "Well you are going to anyway so you might as well just enjoy it". She was funny.

When I woke up I was in hospital, and I had things sticking in me and stuff going from bags into me, and I had all wires and things all over me. I didn't like that and it wasn't comfortable. So I went to sleep again.

When I was asleep the children were there again. They said I could play with them. We laughed and sang and they were funny and it didn't hurt. I used to get out of my body to play with them, and then get back in when I woke up.

My friends on earth sent me lots and lots of cards and stuff they had made at school and my Mummy read them out to me. She was looking different, sort of older, and she was crying when she thought I wasn't looking. Hospitals have a funny smell. Sometimes my Mummy smelt like the hospitals. Sylvia said it was because she was sleeping there on a night. My Daddy was there as well but he went out sometimes and just left Mummy there. She was there all the time.

Then I couldn't wake up properly. I could hear my Mummy and the Doctor talking and I could smell the hospital smell. But I couldn't open my eyes and I couldn't speak. So I went to sleep again and Sylvia said it was time to go with them because they were going to take all the stuff off my body soon, and it would all stop working. So I went with them.

There was a lady with the children. I hadn't seen her before, but then I thought why haven't I seen her because she was there anyway. She said I could stay with the children if I liked.

I didn't want to leave my Mummy and my Daddy and my cat but I didn't like my body hurting and the lady said everyone had tried very, very hard to make it stop hurting, but they couldn't. She showed me a lady and a man who were standing next to my body. The lady was all white, but sort of blue as well. It was lovely standing next to her. It felt all nice and warm, like when you get really, really cold and someone wraps a jacket round you and it feels all cosy. That how she felt.

The man was lovely too. He felt all kind and safe. Like when you get a scare and you're frightened and then Daddy says, "No one can hurt you when I'm here"? Well that's how the man felt. He said he was gong to stay with my Mummy for a while because she was feeling frightened just now.

Then the children took my hands and I came out of my body and I didn't go back in it again. It didn't hurt. It just felt better.

The lady with the children said she would stay with me but that the children would have to go with another lady just for a little while. I didn't mind because everything felt lovely. I don't know all the words to say it, but it was like a summery day, all bright and warm and happy. You know when you wake up and the sun is shining, and there's no school, and you can hear your Mummy downstairs, and the cat is snuggled up next to you, and everything is just right? Well it was like that but better.

So I went with the lady. We went where it got brighter and brighter and brighter. Sort of like going into a dark tunnel only the other way round. I laughed because it felt prickly and funny. And then I came here.

I like it here. Some of the children who came to see me are here too. Tommy isn't though. Tommy is getting ready to do some work and he is going to help children like me who are poorly and whose bodies don't work, so he has to learn how to show them how to come over here.

I come back sometimes to see Mummy and Daddy. But Mummy doesn't see me. She talks to the room that was my bedroom as though I'm still in it though, I hear her, and it's nice because she says she loves me. And she says she won't ever forget me. And she says she is sorry. But she doesn't have to be sorry. She didn't make me poorly. It just happened.

The cat sees me. I like watching his face when he sees me, it's funny. My Daddy sometimes feels me, and sometimes hears me when I talk to him. Then he thinks he has just made it up. But he hasn't. I don't always come and see them, just when it's a good idea. If it's a good idea someone brings me. I can't come on my own; I always have someone with me. Sometimes my friends come too, and sometimes I go with them to see their families. It's good doing that because we know about our friends then. We know why they are them. It's nice. Holly has a dog. We chase him around the garden; and sometimes around the house; and we sit quietly while her Mummy reads a story to her little brother, just like she used to read one to Holly. We like that.

There is lots more stuff to say as well. I'll come back if I can. I like this.

7th September 2004

17 My Mummy Has Lost Herself

My Daddy was the one who cared for us. My Mummy wasn't there, she was 'finding herself' in America. My Daddy used to say he hoped she would find herself soon because he was lost without her. He loved her very much but she wanted her independence.

Daddy said he felt better not having independence. He liked having us in his life. He said we were his little Angels my brother and me. Mummy had another baby, a little girl; but she was very poorly and she went to live with Jesus and the other little Angels. I asked Daddy why she couldn't be a little Angel and stay here like us, but Daddy said he didn't know the answer to that one.

Mummy wasn't the same after that. She was very tired and older somehow and she kept losing her temper a lot and then going upstairs 'for some peace and quiet'. She said Daddy tried to help her but she didn't want anyone near her. The Doctor gave her some tablets but she said she wasn't going down that path. So she went to America instead.

I had a fall in the playground. It wasn't Daddy's fault but he said it was. I hurt my head. They told him afterwards the playground should have had a new floor but Daddy said it was too late now.

I was in hospital for a while but I couldn't speak or walk or eat or anything. I heard someone say, "It would be a far kinder thing to let her go" and I heard Daddy shout "NO" very loudly. But when he wasn't there a Nurse came and said she was going to help me; and she put a pillow over my face and she gave me an injection. Then she pressed down on the pillow really hard. I couldn't struggle and I couldn't shout. So I just sort of went to sleep. I could feel my body going sort of slack but I don't know if that was the injection or the pillow. Anyway I died. The Doctor didn't know what the Nurse had done but he was surprised I had died. The machines should have helped but he said to my father that sometimes Nature knows best and that he should try to be glad that I was not suffering any more.

My Daddy said, "What's happening to me? I was a good father and a loving husband and now two children are gone and my wife is gone too". He cried a lot. I know because I saw him afterwards and my brother was sitting with him. My brother is very sad. He misses me and he misses Mummy. He doesn't really miss the baby because the baby never came home. But he is being very quiet now to be good for Daddy and he doesn't laugh anymore.

Please can someone help my brother and my Daddy, and help my Mummy too. She is still trying to find herself. Now she is looking in Brazil.

18 Pueblo

My name is Pueblo and my Country was very hot. We used to play outside all day and just go home to sleep. We ate outside, and sometimes even slept outside. We didn't have many times when we had to stay inside.

When I was told we were going to live in England I was excited. My heroes came from England – David Beckham and Robbie Williams.

I expected the streets to be full of people like them, and to be able to talk to them just like I can talk to my friends. I could talk to anyone in my village any time I wanted to. But England wasn't like I expected. It was cold for a start, well we moved in October and it was dark on a night, and we had to put heating on in the house, and lights; and we had to eat inside. That was strange to eat inside all the time.

I liked it in England though. But people were not always kind to me because my skin was a little darker than theirs, not much but enough to be noticed. And I couldn't speak much English. I was getting better though. I was learning. And I liked going to school. We did different things than in my school. We learned different subjects, and we had a teacher who had played football when he was younger so he was good.

One day I was going to my home after school had finished, and some bigger boys started calling me names. I didn't understand what the names meant, but they were not nice ones, I could tell that. One of them told me to go back to my Country, which was strange because I know in my Country many people from England had gone to live, so I couldn't see why I shouldn't come this way. But they were shouting and shouting. I just didn't say anything back to them because I didn't know what to say. I was a little frightened but not too much because I wasn't far away from home. Then one of them fired a stone at me from a thing he was carrying. I'm not sure what it was but it hit me on my back. I fell over but I got up again and starting running home. My father came out of the house and shouted at the boys and they ran off. But they didn't run very far because I could still hear them shouting when I went inside.

Next day I went to school again but my mother walked part of the way with me until there were lots of children walking and then she left me to go with them. I was not frightened but I was a little nervous.

On the way home I ran a lot of the way to get home quicker because I knew my mother would be worried. The boys were behind me again and were shouting again. One of them said, "Where's the little boy's Mummy and Daddy to look after him then?", and they all laughed. I couldn't see what they were laughing at because that's what my mother and my father always did. Look after me. That's what all mothers and fathers did isn't it? Then they all started throwing stones at me and one of them hit me on my head. I fell down and all of the boys started laughing and kicking and hitting me. There were a lot of them and I was very frightened. And I was in a lot of pain too. Then

I can remember everything going very dark and the voices sort of faded away into the distance.

I had a feeling I wasn't alone and I was so relieved because I thought that someone had made the boys go away again. Then a feeling of lovely quiet and peace was all around me. I looked around but couldn't see anyone I knew. Then a lady was beside me and she told me to relax and let her take over for a little while. I lay back and it was like I was lying back on soft cushions and it was warm like in my Country. I could almost feel the sun on me and I felt wonderful.

I was trying to see if I had gone back home again, but I couldn't see any houses or any of my friends. I could just feel the warmth like the sun and the feeling of everything being fine.

It was a little while before I found out that I wasn't home in my Country, or even in England, but I was in a new world altogether.

But there were some nice parts. My Grandmamma was there, and my Papa man (you would call him a Grandfather but I always called him Papa man). They were smiling and saying it was beautiful to have their lovely boy to be with them. They said they would look after me until I was settled.

I enjoy being with them, but I miss being with my mother and my father. They have gone back to Spain now, because they don't want what happened to me to happen to my brother or my sister.

They don't hate England; they just don't want to lose any more children.

I wish I had met David Beckham though.

19 The Drummer Boy

I wasn't important, but let them think of me. No one knows me now. Not many did then. I died when a man put a bayonet through me. He wasn't aiming it at me but the man he wanted to kill moved and the soldier was charging and there were lots of people around. I've been told he looked ill when he saw I was dead. I was only 10. I was drumming – keeping the rhythm going but not looking round me, and drumming hard so I could hear that and not the screams. It was the way life was. My Sergeant was dead too.

I saw a man in the village one day who was recruiting. He said what a fine life I could have with a beautiful smart new uniform and a drum all of my own; and that drummers don't have to fight. So I thought it would be a good thing to do. I went home and thought about it. I was supposed to ask my mother but I didn't, and when I got to the group of men and boys that morning the recruit man didn't ask me again so I never said. Anyway there I was standing there banging my drum out of sheer panic and feeling sick because of the noise and the smell, and then I was here.

It was a long time ago and I'm happy where I am, but I never had a chance to say goodbye to my family. My mother realised I had run away to join the army but couldn't find out where or when I had gone over the seas. All in the past now but I regret that. She is over here now of course, and I've seen her a lot; well I used to at first.

No one remembers a poor frightened drummer who wished he had listened to his mother. Still I grew over here and I've had a good time doing so. Now I try and help those children who die because of wars. Some of them are involved, some are not. They are all children. They are all precious. They are all frightened inside, even those who have guns in their hands and shout a lot. They feel scared to pieces inside. They would not be there if adults had not filled their heads with passions and ideals too advanced for their years. I was the same. I know how they feel.

When will we learn not to bring our troubles to rest on the shoulders of our young? You don't see that in the animal kingdom. They teach their young to survive but not to bear grudges. Not to kill for the sake of an icon or a cross or a God. And what God worth following would kill the young. It would make no sense. Kill the young and you kill the future. Without a future there is no one to be the God of.

Blessings to you all and remember me a little please.

17th October 2004

20 War Torn Countries

You talk about war torn Countries. I've heard you. You ask everyone to pray for peace and that the leaders will talk instead of fighting. I wish that had happened in my Country. I was 7 when the bombs fell. No warning. Just now we are here and now we are dead. But at least my family all came over together; all my family - seven brothers and sisters; all wiped out.

My father was in the fields; my mother was already in paradise. She had been ill and she and the new baby went together so my sister took over looking after us. She was 14 then. She had been going to school but she had to leave.

My brothers were allowed to stay at school because it is important for men to be educated but it is not so necessary for women, so my sister left school to look after us. We other girls all helped her. I was then going to school just on a morning and my sister *[Jellef?]* on an afternoon. We shared a place like lots of our girl friends shared with their sisters. Life was not easy for my father. He worked in the fields all day to make enough money to feed us and to let my brothers go to school.

The bombs were to make our Country safe. It wasn't safe for us. It is strange here but we will accustom ourselves to it. My brothers thought they should be in a different place to us but they are not. My sister does not have to be in charge anymore but she says she will always be looking over our welfare.

She is lovely now, all sparkly and happy. She is allowed to learn whatever she wants. Not just subjects suitable for women. She is learning a lot. She says the bombs really did free her.

17th October 2004

21 Biffa's Friend

[Note – this came through on an evening when my male cat Biffa was trying to be the centre of my attention but he was also much more interested in the notebook and pen than usual, and was obviously being 'played with' by someone unseen]

Your cat is funny, we come and play sometimes. We like them all but he is my favourite. He comes over to me when we arrive and I tickle him. He is trying to get me to tickle him now, but I want to talk to you if that is all right with you.

I came here because a boy – well he was a man really – threw a brick off a bridge and it went crash into our car. Daddy swerved with shock because the brick came through the window and hit Mummy in the face. When Daddy swerved we hit another car, and then another car came into the back of our car. And I can't remember how after that I was just here. In a lovely place, but I was very frightened. I was worried about Mummy but they let me go and see her in the hospital and she is going to be pretty again one day but it will take a while. She still doesn't know about me yet though. She is in shock still so they are going to wait till she is stronger.

Karen Wood

When I was very frightened I went to stay with a pretty lady who says she likes having new children and she helps us to grow used to being here and to be happy. She says she knows you and that one day we may see you. I have seen you when we play with your cats but she doesn't mean that. She says you will know.

I am happy now but I would like to be able to tell my Mummy and my Daddy that I am happy. I do miss them. We all miss our Mummies and Daddies. Well the ones of us that knew them anyway. I was very lucky. I had a Mummy and a Daddy who loved me very much. Some people don't have that. I am glad I did.

22 Where Are You?

My story isn't a long one, but I would like to tell it. Help me to write it down so that I can be found amongst so many who are lost.

Our parents don't know what happened to us. They only know they cannot hold us in their arms again. We are gone they think. Well to them we are but we are not gone. We are here. We hear them cry out "Where are you" but we cannot tell them what they want to know. We can only say "We are here".

They wish to know where our earthly bodies are. They wish to know how to find us so that they have what they call closure. I've heard them say it "I have no closure". If it is important then they need it. But we are not closed. We are here.

When they think of their lost child please ask them to say "Where are you now" – not just "Where are you".

We cannot always show them how to find our earthly remains. It would sometimes be impossible and sometimes not wise. But we are not with our earthly bodies, we are here. We can tell you we are happy. We love, we live, we move, we see, we hear, we play, we sing, we dance, we laugh. We can tell you all that. But we have moved on from where we were.

My life was very short in your world. I was born a girl, a great disappointment to my father; a sixth girl. So he gave me to his friend to 'see to'. His friend 'saw to me'.

My mother was told I was given to an English family to bring up as their own. She longs to find the family so that she can see me again. In her heart she fears that this is not true, but her mind tells her it is so. It is better if her mind tells her this. I did not suffer. I was never hungry. I was never cold. But I never felt my mother's arms around me and I never felt the warm sun on my face.

When I hear my mother cry, "Where are you?" I can only say, "I am here".

This lovely little girl was also responsible for "I am Here" in the poetry section

23. Miriam

Hi can I talk to you please. My name is Miriam and I died when I was run over by a bus. I was five years old and I was running after my ball. I didn't wake up but I was in hospital for a long time before I came over here, because my mother couldn't bear to have them turn off all the machines that were keeping me going. They kept my body alive but inside I wasn't really there. I was sort of hovering; not in my body and not in the Spirit World. That's what I wanted to tell people. I wasn't wandering around I was sort of waiting.

It was a long time ago now but I still remember that time of just waiting. A lady was with me and some other children. They stayed with me and we played and sang and danced. But my body was just lying there, and I was still attached to it.

I have heard people in your world saying that 'he went a long time ago; this is just a shell we are keeping alive'. Well I want to tell you that I was still there, just hovering about. But when they turned off the machines I went 'whoosh' over to the tunnel and came into the Spirit World. I was ready. I wanted to go by then because I wanted to move around like the children that came to play with me, and I wanted to be able to go and see my mother at her house instead of sitting quietly by my bedside. I would have liked to get better but my body just wouldn't have mended. It was too broken. And my brain wouldn't have worked properly either, so I wouldn't have been able to do things I had been able to do before. Like reading books and writing, and drawing, and talking even. I wouldn't have been able to use my hands or my legs properly either because the bit of my brain that made that happen didn't work any more.

She was very brave my mother. She wouldn't let them turn off the machines until she was ready, but when she did turn them off she let them use bits of my body to help other children, and that's good. I'm glad she let them do that. Well I didn't need them any more did I?

She stood by my bedside and said, "Goodbye my darling I will always love you", and then she nodded to the Doctor and the Nurse and they pulled out the plugs and things and turned off the machines. And they took all the tubes and sticky things off my body. And then, when my body stopped breathing I was able to go to the Spirit World. You see I had never STOPPED breathing before they put me on the machines to make life easier. If I had stopped I might have gone then but I never did.

I don't blame people. I wasn't in pain or unhappy, I was just hovering around my body, with the silver cord attaching me to it. The cord just sort of evaporated when my body stopped breathing.

I have grown up now in the Spirit World, but I just wanted to tell you about that bit because people don't always get it right. And they should.

Don't worry about me being over here. I am fine. I am helping to look after other young children who are waiting for their bodies to stop working. So I am a bit like the lady who stayed with me. Well I will be when I have finished learning how, at the moment I just go along with another lady, or sometimes a gentleman, who go to stay with a child till they can come over here. I'm not like the children who go to play. I am older than that, but I do talk to the child who is in waiting, and I tell them how it was with me so that they are not frightened when it happens.

Thank you for listening to me. I feel better now I can tell people about me. And about what happened.

24 *Bertram*

Can everyone please send their love to my brother? He thinks it is his fault that I am dead. He thinks he should have been taking better care of me. But he didn't know that I had decided, when I woke up that morning, that I was going to swim in the pool. It wasn't a big pool, and it was covered up when Daddy wasn't there. But Daddy had uncovered it that morning before he left for work, because the man was coming to clean it out. It was full of water when I went outside.

My brother shared a bedroom with me, and usually I woke him up before I got dressed, but this morning I didn't get dressed so I didn't wake him. I just got out of bed very quietly and left the bedroom. I went downstairs and opened the front door. It was easy to open the door because the man to clean the pool was due and Mummy had left the latch up ready for him. I went round the back and there was the pool. The light was shining on it from the sun and the water was all sort of sparkly. It was very pretty and I wanted to swim in it.

My Daddy had always said that we must never go in it on our own. But I thought, "I won't be on my own very long because the pool man is coming". So I climbed down the steps into the water. It was very cold but it was lovely. I could swim a little bit but not a lot. We had a shallow bit and a deeper bit. So I swam in the shallow bit. But I was in the middle when I got tired. Usually when I got tired Daddy grabbed me and helped me to the side. But Daddy wasn't there. And the pool man wasn't there. And Mummy was at the other side of the house. So I drowned.

I can't remember the actual drowning bit. But I can remember a sort of whooshing whistling sort of feeling and everything being very bright and warm and then I was being held by a lady who said, "Hello little boy, you look a nice boy. Now just stay quietly a little while till you are properly awake".

I asked where Mummy was and the lady said Mummy was just going out to hang out the clothes. I said, "I was swimming". The lady smiled but didn't say anything. Then I realised that I couldn't go to Mummy and I got a bit frightened. The lady sort of cuddled me and I went all warm and sleepy. That kept happening. I got a little frightened and the lady made me feel warm and sleepy and safe. That's the main thing. I felt very safe.

My Mummy was very upset and she says she will never get over it. But she will one day. Because one day she will come over here herself and see how nice it is. We can play and play and play. And laugh and laugh and laugh. I live with a man who laughs a lot and a lady who looks all sparkly. There are a lot of us but we are all safe. No one hurts us. We can go in the sea and right under it, but when we go we hold hands so that we don't get lost.

We hold hands a lot. I usually hold hands with Jimmy on one side of me and Paula on the other side. Jimmy is my best friend. He came over here when he was two and the hole in his heart leaked. Something like that anyway. Paula came here when she was a baby and fell asleep and forgot to breathe. Jimmy says she must have been very silly forgetting to breath, but Stanley (the man who looks after us) says it was a good thing for us because we love having Paula living with us.

She is my bestest girl friend. Jimmy says she is OK for a girl, but he likes her a lot really. They are good friends but he says she is very silly sometimes. Paula says Jimmy is very good but he should have more laughing. I like being with them both.

My brother still misses me and still blames himself; but it was my idea to swim and I didn't tell him and anyway he was asleep so he couldn't see.

My mother is sure it was her fault, but it wasn't because she didn't know I was going to swim.

Daddy has filled in the pool now. I am sorry about that but they all say they could not swim in it again. They are going to grow a garden just for me. Can you send them love please?

My name is Bertram.

25 The Designer

They said I should have been born a girl. They were cruel. It was because I liked to dress my sister's dolls. The clothes that came with them were so badly made I used to make new ones. My mother had lots of material around the house. She showed me how to sew and I used to just know in my head how to cut them out and put them together… My sister used to be so pleased with them – I didn't want to play with the dolls, just see them better dressed.

I didn't like climbing trees or playing fights or playing football, but that didn't make me a bad person did it? I never hurt anyone. My mother was always very good. She used to say, "Just ignore them they have none of your fine spirit. They will never amount to anything". But it was hard.

I didn't want to play with girls. I was happy in my own company. Many days would go by and I wouldn't leave my room. I just sat and read or drew or made clothes for my sister's dolls, and sometimes for my sister's friends' dolls. They liked them.

If a dress was on television, worn by an actress or a model, my sister would say, "Can you make me one like that"? Sometimes

I could but really I preferred making the ones out of my head. My mother said I had a great talent and would make a name for myself. I didn't want to make clothes for my sister or myself but my mother said that was fine. My imagination could have a freer reign with the dolls, and perhaps when I was older I may design for women rather than children. She said my designs were excellent and that they were not suitable for young girls anyway. She said my work was exquisite.

That's all very well but whenever I left the house I was taunted and jeered by the other boys. They called me names I couldn't understand. But I don't think I was whatever it meant. I was just artistic. I could see designs in my head and I could put them down on paper and I could make the clothes appear.

I loved the holidays because I could draw and sew all day. It never occurred to my sister to buy clothes for her dolls at the shops. She said mine were far better. My mother said I was a sensitive soul, whatever that meant. I don't know if I was or not. I just know I had ideas in my head. My mother used to say "Mark my words that boy will go far".

I was walking home one day from school when some boys set on me. They started by calling me names but I was used to that, so they then began to throw clods of mud and sticks at me. I tried hurrying home but some of them were standing at the front of me and some at the back. They started pushing me and punching me. Then I fell to the ground and one of them stamped on my hands. I heard the noise of bones breaking before I felt the pain. The boys ran off when they realised I was badly hurt. They weren't really as bad as they must sound. They were just being tough in front of each other. When I got home I couldn't open the door because my hands were so painful and were swelling, but also they were a funny shape. I called out to my mother to come and help me.

My sister heard me and opened the door. She screamed and ran for my mother. She called an ambulance. I had a cut on my face which needed stitches; I had two broken ribs which I hadn't even noticed - but my hands!

The Doctor told my mother this was a job for the Police as well as for him. I went straight to surgery but they couldn't do much to help at that point. The Doctor called for another Doctor, a specialist in bones and plastic surgery. He said if I was lucky they would be able to save my left hand and it should work fairly well, but my right hand was a different thing. The bones were broken in so many places it may not work much; but that he would do his very best and that it would take a long time and would be painful.

I couldn't dress myself, or wash myself, or feed myself and I had another operation to put in a catheter so I didn't have to go to the toilet. I had other operations too. My stomach and abdomen were in a mess too but it was my hands that were my main problem. I was horrified to look at them. They were ugly. They were all out of shape. They looked like old man's hands.

The Police came. They wanted to know who had done it and why. They were very nice and kind. I knew the names of some of the boys but not all of them. There were no witnesses but they took my clothes and they took samples from my nails. They did that when I was asleep before an operation because it was too painful for me. They proved which boys it was but they couldn't do much to them, because of their age they said. But they did have to go to Court and they did have to face me. The parents of one of them brought him to the hospital to see what he had done. He was feeling sick when he went away.

As I said, they weren't evil, they just were a crowd; and a crowd is different to a person on their own.

I got an infection in my lungs. One of my ribs had gone through it you see. I can't remember much else.

I heard a nurse say I would have to fight this one very hard, and that I must not give up. But I wasn't a fighter I was an artist. I didn't know how to fight.

I just kept lying in bed with tubes everywhere crying inside because of my hands. Because I knew I wouldn't be able to sew again or draw and that the ideas in my head would have to stay there.

So I didn't fight. I gave up. Was that bad of me?

Now I am learning to help other people have ideas. It will take a long time to learn but I don't mind. I am not in pain and I can create now; in lots of different ways. It's peaceful here.

The boys have to go back to Court but I don't care anymore. I'm not there in that body am I? My mother keeps crying about a great talent wasted by thugs. One day she might find out that I'm not wasted, that they say I can do good from here. One of the ones who help to make the world a more beautiful place. I'd like that. I hope I can.

26 Marcus

I was born on Christmas Day, December 25th 1942. That would make me old now but on May 17th 1943 I died. My parents were very upset of course; well you would hardly be surprised at that would you? But they just got on with their lives.

You see I was the fourth child they had lost; none lived more than two years. They were never blessed with seeing their young offspring grow to adulthood, but do you know they still remained two of the happiest people you could wish to meet. They loved each other, they loved their house, which was small but catered for their needs. They loved their families, adored their many nieces and nephews and were never bitter. How could this be when they had endured so much sorrow and hardship?

Because they believed in the path they trod. It was not so much that they had faith. Oh they attended their local parish Church regularly, and indeed our earthly bodies, my brothers, my sister and I, were all buried in the Churchyard. But their surety came in the certain knowledge that life was eternal, and that one day we would all be reunited.

So, to tell you my story briefly, as I said I was a very small child, a babe in fact, when I went to Spirit or, as I prefer to say, when I was born into the world in which I live. Yes I was born into this world. That is how I truly think of it; a beginning not an ending.

I was met on all sides with people who gave me love, kindness and, very precious to one so young, their full attention.

At all stages as I grew up I was given all the attention I needed or wanted. I was never cold or hungry for food of course, but as my spirit grew I yearned more and more for knowledge. At every stage I was encouraged to ask questions, and every question was unfailingly answered. Sometimes the answer was not to the question I *thought* I had asked but I learned as I grew older to be careful how I phrased the question, because I was not given information I had not requested. There were two reasons for that: -

1. I had not asked, and,
2. If you do not ask the question you are not ready for the answer.

Was my childhood happy I can hear some of you asking? Well yes, thank you, it was very enjoyable. Do not run away with the idea that because we grew in this world we were perfect angels - far from it. We were encouraged to think for ourselves and to explore any point we thought about. So when, as a young boy, I wanted to know about the many creatures that live under the water in your world I, along with others who were also curious, were brought back to your world to explore under the seas, in the lakes and reservoirs. I was introduced to the inhabitants too numerous to mention at this time, including some so small you would never see them with your human eyes. I learned how they lived, how they interacted with their own kind and others, and how they all formed a chain to keep the world a fit and healthy environment. Of course I was also shown how mankind was not working in the same way. You think it a modern day problem, well it was in full effect when I was a child but man was a little late in noticing.

I was also taken to see the animals who had left your world and come to ours. They live in an environment that pleases them. It does not need to please us. You may have heard of the 'animal kingdom' in the Spirit World we frequent? Well to explain just a little, they do not choose to live in the same area, if you like to call it that, as us, because they are happy with their own and on their own. You do not choose to share a house with elephants or kangaroos on earth do you? And they would not be happy with you either. It is the same. They have no ill feelings towards us, indeed they do not always notice that we exist, and there is no need for them to do so. So we visited, we learned, and we left them in peace.

I learned to visit my family, my mother and my father. They did feel our presence and they smiled as they remembered each of us, for we often visited together my siblings and I.

My mother is now with us in our world having lived a full life, and having passed to our world as a contented person. My father is still with your world but will soon join his loving wife.

Be not sad for those who go before. Be only joyful for the life we maintain, and be glad of the memories, and be happy with your path.

Who could ask for more? I leave you with the love and blessings of all of those who love you and are loved by you.

One thought more I would like to leave with you my friends. On the morning that the world unites in their many ways of being happy, and celebrating your world, do not let your thoughts linger on what might have been. Look forward to what *could* be. Far more satisfying.

Be peaceful and be happy.

Marcus and his siblings Miranda, John, Edward

27 How Did I End Up Over Here?

How did I end up over here? I was playing in the garden with my dog, Hannibal I called him, and he was a Scottish terrier I think, Daddy used to say he was a mixed bag but Mummy said he was beautiful.

Anyway we were playing in the garden; I was throwing the ball and he was running after it and then picking it up and dropping it, and I had to go and get it off him so I could throw it again. I was laughing and Hannibal was barking and wagging his tail.

Then I saw something else on the ground. It was a funny dirty colour and I was curious so I picked it up. It was about the size of a large potato but I didn't know what it was so I carried it into the kitchen to show my mother. She took one look at it and told me to put it down. I asked why but she just screamed "Throw it away!" I was fiddling with the thing I had found and then ………I don't remember anything else I just came here.

It was a shock because I hadn't been ill and I hadn't been run over so I didn't know why I wasn't at home any more. I didn't like being away from my Mummy and Daddy and I wanted to go home. Maria, the lady who talked to me first said she knew I did, but that I would soon be sleepy and wouldn't mind so much. She also said that no one was going to harm me and that everyone here would just love me and look after me as though they were my new family, which was OK in its way, but I liked my old family best and I wanted them back.

So then I sort of did get sleepy and everything seemed to be better, and I didn't feel energetic enough to worry about anything. I just sort of went to sleep. You know the feeling just as you are dropping off to sleep and everything is fine, and you just feel cosy and warm and safe. That's how I felt.

I don't know how long I was like that but eventually I felt curious about where I was and not so frightened. I don't mean I was happy but I was curious and I wanted to see where I was. I still wanted to go back home but I wasn't frightened of where I was. It seemed safe and everything.

A lady came and talked to me, not Maria, another lady and said she would get Maria to come and see me. I thought that would take a long time but there Maria was, I can't remember her coming she was just there. She smiled, and she had a lovely smile, and said, did I want to come and see the children I would be staying and playing with? They were just learning to sing a song and I could join in if I liked.

The song was all about birds and them singing like we were trying to sing, but it was funny and I liked it. They were nice the other children. One boy had just arrived in the group the same as I did, so I talked to him and he said he had just decided to see what was happening before he decided if he was going to stay. I said where was he going to go if he didn't stay and he said he didn't know but he was just looking around. He sounded tougher than me so I didn't say anything. It hadn't occurred to me not to stay. I asked Maria if there was anywhere else to go if we didn't like it. She said she hoped we would like it, but if we were unhappy there she would find us another group to be with. I did like it and eventually so did Endean. He just liked to argue a lot, and ask loads and loads of questions which he thought no one would be able to answer so that he would look clever. They just made a funny joke out of it and said – "Oh you got me that time I will find out". And they always DID find out the answer, so he gave up, and he did try to be the boss out of him and me, but I let him sometimes and other times when he was being silly I just thought about being with someone else and I went and was with someone else in the group.

We learned lots and lots of things, but it didn't seem hard work because it was always fun, and we didn't get tired or have to stop and eat. We did sort of rest though, it seems strange saying it because we didn't lie down or anything we just well sort of rested.

When I am a little older I will decide if I want to help other people or not. We don't have to but it seems silly just to do nothing, and we know a lot of people need help. Not just in my world that I live in now, but in your world too. There are lots and lots and lots of ways we can help each other. Just like there are lots and lots and lots of ways you can help each other too

If I decide to help people in your world, I will start by coming back now and again, I did come back sometimes to see my family, but I didn't really like it very much because Mummy kept crying and Daddy went and lived with another lady. Then Mummy came over to this world, and I see her a lot, but she has to sleep a lot too, she goes into a sort of bubble to make her feel better, then when she comes away from there she comes to see me for a little while, but not for ever and ever, she is not ready for that yet, and I am happy in my life as it is, but I like it when Mummy is there too.

Daddy is happier than he was but not really happy, he knows he did wrong to not live with Mummy any more, but Maria says that sometimes people just do silly things because they don't know what else to do to feel better. Daddy loved me and he loved Mummy really, but he had the thought in his head that if he had been there I would have just put the thing I was holding down quietly. And he thought Mummy should not have screamed at me. But Mummy was frightened. I know that now.

Oh – when Mummy came over to this world, Daddy took Hannibal to live with him, so that was good. Hannibal is happy.

I am happy now too. No one needs to be frightened of living here. Maria says it's much safer than your world. I think she is right.

28 I Swam With The Dolphins Mum

Hiya Mum, you won't believe what I've been up to today. Well, you know when I was ill, and they asked me what I wanted to do before I finished on earth (they used a lot of words to not say "before I died" didn't they?).

Well if you remember I said I wanted to swim with the dolphins. They had it all arranged but then my blood went wonky and I couldn't go could I?

Well you see, when I got here they asked me if there was anything I really, really wanted to do to make myself feel more at home. So, of course, I said I wanted to swim with the dolphins.

So a group of us came and we went right out to sea and swam with wild dolphins, not the ones in the pools and stuff, but right out at sea where the dolphins are because they like being there. They like people too but they like being out at sea. So that's where we swam with them, and it was lovely. We could ride on their backs and swim alongside them, and laugh with them, and they laughed with us too because we could sort of understand what they wanted and they could understand what we wanted and they were lovely. So we may go back and do it again one day because everyone enjoyed it.

I like it here but of course I really wanted to stay with you and Dad, and with Ben and Abigail, but my blood was wonky and it got more and more wonky and the chemo monster didn't make it stop being wonky so I had to come here.

Don't be sorry for me, just love me and keep on loving me because that's what I feel most. When people send me their love, it's sort of like a wave or a wind and it comes right over you and under you and you feel all lovely. When people are sad we feel that too but usually there is love mixed up with the sadness, but its better when it's just love and smiles and not sadness.

When you think of me can you smile please? I like to see you smiling and I like to see you playing with the dog. Oh and another thing. When you play with the dog and you laugh, please don't stop and think to yourself, how can I laugh when she isn't here? It's OK to laugh honestly; it helps us if our parents are laughing.

I know it isn't easy for you. I know you want me back, I can feel that too. I know you think I am with you all the time and I am there when it's a good idea but I am not there all the time because I am settling in to where I am now. And I have a lot of new friends to play with and to talk to and to run with. And I DON'T have to stand still and then lie down every time I have been running any more.

There is a man here who says he knows you, and says he will look after you. He isn't a guide but he has been with the family while I have been ill and when they were getting used to me being over here, and he says he knows you are not ready for him

Children of the Light

to move on yet, but that you will be one day, and then he will go and help another family while their child is poorly.

Can you tell Ben that I read his letter he put on my grave? It was lovely but he should put it inside something next time because it got all soggy and blew away. We giggled when we were reading it because it was blowing away all the time. But we knew what it said because we felt him and read his thoughts when he was writing it.

So please keep thinking of me when you want to. Please don't feel guilty when you feel happy, and please don't spend all that money on buying things to put on my grave, because I know you don't have much money, and I don't want you spending it on things for me when I can't take them over here. I have an idea. Just look at something in a shop and think of me, and then I can pick it up just the same as if you have spent the money and put it on my grave. I will get just as much fun out of it I promise you.

I do love it when Abigail draws pictures and says they are for me. Tell her to keep on doing it, and to put them on the wall in her bedroom where the light goes twinkley sometimes and she thinks it's me talking to her.

I like it when she does that because she isn't frightened at all and she just talks to me as though I am still in the room with her. Sometimes I AM in the room with her, but sometimes I pick up her thoughts and come closer to her.

Its good being able to go where I want and do what I want, as long as it doesn't put me in any problems. We don't get shouted at but we are very closely looked after so that we don't get lost or go near people who won't love us and look after us properly.

Karen Wood

We have been told we can keep on coming down to see people, and to learn from people on earth, because that will help us when we go to find something to work with, to help people on earth when we are older.

I have a couple more years yet before I can do that

29 Caroline

Hello I wanted to come and talk to you about what happened to me, but I don't know how to do it, so I have told this lady instead.

I was only 5 when I came over here. I wasn't ill, well I don't think I was anyway, but my head went all funny and my brain forgot to tell my lungs to breath. Wasn't that silly of it? So I came over here and now I don't have a brain and I don't have any lungs so nothing can forget. I'm not upset about it, but my mother was VERY upset. She cried and cried and cried and she screamed at my father that it must be his fault because he was looking after me while she was having a break with her friends

My Daddy was very upset too, but was more upset because my mother thought it was his fault. You see I shouldn't really have been born at all. My mother was very young, and my father was supposed to be with another lady. So when I came along my Granny said it was "Inconvenient to say the least" and told my mother she would have to find somewhere else to live.

My mother moved into a flat by herself and she was living there when I was born. My Daddy did help her a lot but was still living with another lady so it was very complicated.

Sometimes my Mummy's friend would come and stay the night and my Mummy would go out and have a break with her friends. Sometimes Daddy came and sat with me. I just went to sleep whoever was there.

I had a lot of other Daddies. One was Daddy John and another was Daddy David, but they only seemed to be a Daddy for a little while and then they stopped and someone else became a Daddy. But my real Daddy was just Daddy and didn't have another name on the end.

He was there even when the Daddy names were there sometimes. I never saw the lady he lived with when he wasn't seeing me though. She is nice, I've been to see Daddy since I have been here and she is very pretty and very clever. Daddy really does love her, but he never talks about me to her. I don't know why.

Anyway, I came over here because my body forgot to work. I wasn't scared, I just thought my Mummy had gone away and left me with a friend again, but that this time she forgot to pick me up again. She had done that before, and I was with another lady for nearly a week before Mummy came for me.

But now I can go back and see Mummy any time I want to, and she doesn't have to keep going away for a break anymore. She is very sad though, and says she loves me much more than she thought she did, and that she wishes she had spent more time with me.

It sounds as if my Mummy wasn't a good Mummy but she was. She loved me, and she always made sure I was clean and fed, and always made sure I had someone looking after me, and she was still very young when I came over here.

My Granny never looked after me, and now that I am over here she says "It's all for the best" and has told my Mummy she may come back home to live again, but my Mummy doesn't want to.

My Daddy is very sad, and says the light in his life has gone out. I don't know what he means by that because the lights in his bedroom all work, and in his living room, because I have checked them all. They wobbled when I tried to turn them off but they didn't go off properly. They were all on when I left. Daddy was surprised because he hadn't put ALL the lights on.

I don't do that sort of thing with my Mummy because she would be very frightened. My Daddy says he knows it was me trying to contact him. I wasn't, I was just trying to see if his lights had gone out like he said.

When I go to see my Mummy I just try to tell her I am all right. Sometimes I think she hears me but mostly she just keeps on crying.

I don't go to see my Granny because she wouldn't want me to anyway. She just wants to forget I was ever born, put it all behind her she keeps saying. I don't think my Granny is very happy though. She never smiles inside herself like most people do. Do you do that? I bet you do. Most people when we look into their hearts have a happy side of them, but my Granny doesn't seem to have one.

I have to go now, we are all going to go and play with a cat that has come over to our world and is feeling lonely. He likes children and he will feel better if we play with him. We like to make people and animals feel better. It makes us feel better too.

Bye bye - Oh my name is Caroline.

(28th May 2006)

30 Jemima

My name is Jemima and I left your world when I was just five years old. I am older now but I still remember well the day of my passing.

My mother had taken me to buy some new shoes for school. I was to travel a few days later to my first ever Boarding School. It may seem young to most of you that I was to go to a Boarding School at five years old, but my parents were due to work in another Country, and it was thought best that I would be safe and well and cared for at my new school, rather than travelling with them to a Country not classed as so civilised as our own.

We were crossing a road when a bus driver swerved to avoid a cyclist, and collided with a car. Who knows who was to blame, the result was the same, my mother and I both entered the world I now call my home.

My mother was very shocked, and I was just unsure what was happening. At such a young age you adapt more quickly. Part of me wondered if this new strange surrounding was my new school. Part of me wondered why my mother was there with me. It was expected that my uncle would arrive the next morning to take me to the school you see, he lived very close and was the reason that particular school had been chosen.

However, although I was close to my mother I was not totally with her in these new surroundings. That may seem strange but you have to remember that my mother was very shocked, and very confused, and not really capable of looking after herself let alone a young charge such as myself.

Other hands looked after me, made sure I felt safe, and comforted me when I was scared, or overwhelmed.

Eventually my mother was led away to begin her new life, and I was led away to begin mine. Oh, I saw a lot of my mother, but she did not have the total control of my wellbeing. It is so much more organised than that, although she was with me a lot.

When you hear of your loved ones saying that they have the young child who has passed with them, they do not mean that they are bringing them up alone. They mean that they visit them a good deal, and that at that particular time when they are in communication with you, the child is with them. But there are other people who have put on hold the chance to develop their Spirits, to prepare them to move on to another plain, so that they can dedicate their time to looking after those young pure souls who have made the journey earlier than would normally be assumed.

I grew to maturity in a safe group of likeminded youngsters, whom I will forever think of as part of my family. Cared for, spiritually and emotionally nourished by those lovely people I have already mentioned.

My mother, lovely beautiful soul that she is, came often to see me, but it was some time before she was capable of understanding what had happened to either of us, and she did feel for a long while that it was somehow her fault that I was there, and she was concerned at how her husband, my father, would be able to cope without her, or indeed without me, and she feared that he would blame her for my loss.

In fact my father blamed himself for both our losses. It was, of course, not at all any fault of his, or possibly of anyone. Cars, buses and cyclists are a combination to be feared on a busy road. I prefer to think that I was unfortunate, rather than a victim.

The bus driver, and the car driver, and indeed the cyclist, all had times when they blamed themselves, each other, my mother, and sometimes me, for what had happened. This is natural, the human mind will always try to analyse a situation and try to find a solution which is easier to live with than one in which self blame has to be acknowledged.

I am now a matured Spirit, in that I am no longer living with the group of youngsters I grew with. I do not work as such, I decided that I wanted to have some time to myself, to decide what I wished to do, but I will choose something one day. It is by no means compulsory, but eternity is a very long time, and to spend that just aimlessly drifting must be very mundane. So I shall work. I feel I am drawn to some form of communication with your world, although of course I have not the knowledge or the advancement to be a Guide or even a helper. I may work with a circle, that would be interesting. I may even work with a healing worker on this side, learning how to help those in your world dedicated enough to try to help others less able than themselves. I have not totally decided.

I cannot say that I have come here today to give you deep and meaningful advice on how to run your lives. That would be very wrong of me as I am not a suitable person to tell you this. I have not the experience of living in your world, or the knowledge enough yet from living in my own.

I can, however, tell you that there is no need to fear the transition from one world to another, that when you arrive here when your earthly journey is done, you will be met with love and help. That for each person the transition is slightly different, because it will depend on how shocked, or ill, or under what circumstances you arrived. There will be someone here who will understand. It would be of no use being welcomed by someone who had no knowledge or experience of what you have just encountered now would it?

I must leave you now my friends, but please enjoy your lives, live them as well as you can, and hopefully you will achieve all that you wish, provided of course that what you wish is good for the planet, and for those around you too.

Goodbye my new friends. Take care and be good to each other.

Jemima

31 Andreaus

Hello everyone. My name is Andreaus. It isn't my real name, that was lost long ago but I like to be called Andreaus.

How are you all? I lived on what you call your world a long, long time ago. I left when I was young, and so I feel that talking to this lady is appropriate.

I did not die in battle, or as a result of illness, or because another person wished me ill. I died because I was foolish enough to try to beat a lioness to her food.

I was hungry you see. I had been living on my own for a year or so, living on my wits and on my instincts, which were usually good. I had once been part of a large and integrated family, but my father and I had been out hunting, and he had lost an engagement with a boar. I was too young to be able to find my way back to my people, although I did try. From the information I have now I was not too far away from them when I saw a small animal, similar to an antelope, drinking at the river. I crept up behind it, hoping to be able to be at the correct position before she spotted me. I would then have brought her to the ground and beaten her head with the rocks I had already placed nearby, as I always did at any river. I had no other weapon you see, I had learned to craft one or two, but they had broken before the day I am relating to you.

I was so busy watching the small animal that I failed to notice the larger, more able hunter to my left. As I moved close I was suddenly aware of the small animal's start of fear, which did not seem to be related to me. Next I was aware of warm, rather acrid breath and a searing pain on my back. I cannot honestly say I put up a brave fight. I fell to the ground and I remember a short period of pain and nothing more for a while.

My father was standing nearby, smiling and holding out his arms. He told me that he had walked with me many a mile since we had been parted. It did not surprise me. We were taught as a people that those who went before us did simply that. We respected all life, but knew that we had to eat. We would not kill unless we were hungry, and then the whole animal was used in one way or another. Well, it was when the family was altogether. On my own I simply ate what I could, used what materials I needed and buried the rest, or left it in the sun for the scavengers if they were about. That way they left me alone a little longer.

This may seem strange to you; that we had no dwellings, which I know you call houses, and no material things. The computers you use nowadays are wonderful, but they do not seem to have led you to understanding what you have around you. They do not make you kinder to each other, or to the animals that still remain in your world.

You seem not to sit on a morning and glory in the day ahead. I was taught to sit very still when I first arose, to smell and to savour the world which was mine. This of course also taught you what animals or other visitors had been near your space, and which ones were still nearby. We relied heavily on our senses. Yes all six of our senses. We knew by instinct some things, others we were taught.

I have many happy memories still of my time in your world. But many, many, more of my time in the world I now inhabit, and which I would not change.

I have come back several times to see the places where I lived, but they do not seem the same any more, or perhaps they seemed large to me because I was small.

Living, and learning in this world, we see the dangers, and the tribulations that surround you in your day to day existence. I often wonder who has the most danger. You do not need to forage each day for your food, and certainly a passing like mine would not be the common occurrence that it was then. You see we lived on our instincts, but possibly not as closely as the lioness did. I learned afterwards that she had youngsters to feed, and so her need was greater than mine. If I had seen her I would have left the prey for her. Not simply because she had young, but because even as a sapling I knew she would have been a better hunter than I was, and hungry I may have been, but so foolish I was not.

I am finding it more difficult than I at first thought to use this method of speaking, but I am grateful for the opportunity I have of communicating.

It is good to be able to let you know my story, I have enjoyed that, but mainly I wished to be able to tell you all how much you are loved, by this world I mean. Not just by myself, though of course that is the case too.

This beautiful wonderful Spirit World which I inhabit, is so closely linked to your own that sometimes I wonder you do not feel us around you, so near are we. I have heard some of you wonder how it can be that you call and we hear. That is because we are attuned to your needs, and to your thoughts, as we are to each others.

In this world if we need to speak to one another we have only to think of the person we need to speak to, and we are either together, or we are in communication. It sounds easy but it is not quite so easy to adjust to. There is a certain amount of having to believe the evidence which is before you, but not before eyes or ears, as you have been used to trusting. This period passes and we accept the way things are.

As your loved ones journeyed to this world, sometimes they expected to see one thing, sometimes another, and I am always fascinated to watch the dawning of the realisation that we all live amicably together, whatever creed, Country, belief, colour indoctrination or stereotype we had accepted in our earthly travels. Each group does of course gravitate to those with similar ideas and ideals to their own, that is natural, but eventually curiosity leads them to stretch their limitations, until they finally realise that this world in fact HAS no limitations. Imagine that if you can, a people who do not mind what you believe, what you hope for, what you strive for, what you know or do not know, but who see you as a separate person, and love you for your likes, your dislikes, and your shortcomings.

I hope that one day, when your time upon that world you call your home is over, you will love this world as I do. There is no lovelier way to spend your day, or your night, or whatever time you like, it makes no difference here, with outstanding beauty, with people of a like mind to yourself, and others of a different persuasion, in talking and discussing, and learning from each other, with no interruption because of working days, or needing to feed, or sleep or study. Just to be able to finish a discussion to its conclusion.

I do nowadays have a little of my existence taken up by trying to help a young man on his path to Spiritual fulfillment. At the moment that takes only a little of my time, but later it will take more, and the young man will unfold his potential and be able to bring the Worlds even closer and more accessible. This is work I have chosen, and the young man will make his own decision, though, of course, I do sincerely hope he chooses to work with us. I am sure he will do so, but it must be his own unequivocal choice and not influenced by anything I say or do.

Thank you for your patience as I have unfolded some of my thoughts to you. May you live the life you wish deep inside your hearts for yourselves, which is not of course the life your head wishes for you.

Take, please, the blessings and the love of this world, and use the information I have given you as you feel is best for you.

Good bye my friends, and be safe in the knowledge that you are well loved and well blessed.

32 *Tim*

My name is Tim and I am five years old. At least I WAS five years old when I came here. We have two birthdays you know; one when we are born to our Mummies and one when we come here. We have parties both times although not like parties with you when we had cake and bouncy castles and ice cream and stuff.

We play games and sing and laugh lots and lots and lots and it's really cool. My Mummy used to get very worried every time I had a party or went to one in case I ate the wrong foods because I used to be ill if I did.

She used to send me with a bag of stuff I could eat which was nice but I wanted to eat the same as everyone else. So just sometimes I used to sneak something off the plates on the tables and eat it when no one was looking. Sometimes I got away with it but one time I had a bowl of something that was my friend's but he didn't like. It was made of chocolate and biscuits, but it must have had some nuts in it as well because my mouth went all swollen and then I couldn't breathe and then I hurt in lots of places, and then I was in hospital and people were shouting and giving me needles and things.

Then everything went quiet and I heard some children laughing. I could hear them before I could see them, and I heard a lady's voice saying "Hello Timmy we have come to see you". The children were nice and they laughed and talked to me and said I was coming with them to be their new friend.

The lady told me that I didn't have to worry about not eating nuts and things any more. It wasn't just nuts but they were the worst. Then she said that we could go now and we would have some fun when I was ready.

I was a bit frightened and wanted my Mummy at first. Then I wanted my Daddy, and then I just wanted to be at home. I wished I hadn't eaten my friend's food and that I had done what my Mummy said and just eaten what she gave me. But it was too late and I was not in my body any more. I can't remember leaving my body but I can remember the moment when I realised that I had died. It was when one of the children sort of floated around the room and I asked her how she did it. She told me that I could do it as well if I liked and she showed me how and held my hand. I said I didn't know I could do that and she said – well you couldn't do it before when you were in your body. Your body was too heavy to float in the air but now you aren't in your body you can do lots more things.

I couldn't understand why I wasn't in my body but the lady said that I had had to get out of it because it wasn't going to work any more, and that I was better off without it now.

The children came with the lady and me for a while, but then they sort of went and I couldn't remember seeing them go they just weren't with us any more and the lady and I were on our own. That was fine though because she was a lovely lady. I don't remember ever hearing her name but it didn't matter. I felt safe and nice with her. I wasn't ever frightened of her. I was frightened, but not of her or of anyone but just frightened because I still didn't really know what was happening.

The lady and I were together for a little while, and I cant really remember how we got here, I remember lots of light but that's all – it's very light here anyway but I think I am more used to it now than I was so it doesn't seem quite so bright as it did.

Lots of ladies and gentlemen seemed to be there but it all seemed very safe. I didn't worry about where I was; it was a little like the first day at school or the first day you went to see some relatives that you hadn't known before. You wanted to be on your best behaviour but you didn't really want to be there. Everything was interesting, and everyone was kind and smiley and nice. A man told me I was a very brave boy and that I was obviously a very nice boy and that my Mummy and Daddy must be lovely people to have helped me be so good. That made me a little sad because my Mummy and Daddy weren't there and I wanted to be with them, especially my Mummy. I really wanted a hug at that time. One of the ladies gave me a hug thought, and it helped. It wasn't a hug like you give each other on earth. She just sort of made me feel all over like you feel inside when your Mummy gives you a hug. It was funny. I giggled and she giggled with me and gave me a wink.

I was with the lady that gave me a hug for quite a while, I don't know how long because we don't have clocks and things here, and anyway I was just learning to tell the time so I wouldn't have known anyway.

So now I live with lots of children, and we have lots of good times, and learn a lot. I like learning here. I had just started school before I came here, but it wasn't as nice as this. It was nice though. There wasn't anything I didn't like when I was with my Mummy and my Daddy and my body, apart from not being able to eat the same food as everyone else; but here its really good and funny and we can run and run and run and laugh and laugh and smile and ask questions, and no one is too tired to answer them, and you don't have to go to bed because you don't get tired yourself. We do have times when we are quiet though.

I am going now because I have been told it is time. I am going to see my Mummy today but they said I could tell my story first. We like telling our stories and we know people like listening to them so that's good.

Bye everyone.

33. The Inhaler

I see you have an inhaler. I had one but I needed more. The Doctor felt it would not be in my best interests to have any more medication. It would have fought or counteracted with other medication. I had a variety of illnesses, all centred upon my chest. Asthma, Cystic Fibrosis, I had suffered from Pneumonia, often bronchial problems. I was beginning to be more and more dependent upon an increasing number of drugs. The Doctor decided on this occasion to try a different form of help. I was already taking a course of exercises, I was having acupuncture, and I was taking herbal concoctions my aunt got for me. The Doctor suggested I try a gentleman he had recently met who was what he, the Doctor, called 'a Faith Healer'. This was a very courageous step for a modern day Doctor to suggest, but my parents by that time were willing to try any method. The problem occurred with the fact that this so called Faith Healer charged a great amount of money. My father was a good hard working man, but he did not earn enough to be able to pay for the Faith Healer. He took a drastic action, and removed some funds from a deposit account at his place of work. I had the treatment from the man; who actually was not a good man and did not have any helpers working with him; and so there was no improvement.

Of course as you would expect, my father's desperate measures were discovered, and he lost his job. My father was so thrown out of his mind, not only by the fact that he had been tricked by the man the Doctor had recommended. He could not live with his thoughts, and so he took his car and simply drove it over a cliff.

My mother was unable to cope with the loss of my father, the shortage of money, and my ever increasing illnesses. She mixed my medication with something the Doctor had given her to make her sleep, having saved them. I simply slipped into sleep and didn't wake up. Apparently they did try to revive me but I don't remember any of that. My mother then hung herself.

We are all together now, most of the time anyway. We needed to be together to help us settle, and my mother and I both felt that my father needed to know that we wanted to be with him. Please don't feel badly towards my father, or my mother. They are good people and they are suffering about the turn of events. I love them both dearly. I cannot say more yet, but I will return if you would allow.

(Of course I said yes)

Goodbye and thank you.

34. Advent

Advent. Four weeks before Christmas, or rather four Sundays before; a special time for my mother. It is the anniversary of the day my father decided to live with another lady. It may seem strange to you that my mother chooses to celebrate this day. Of course it is a day not a date, the date changes. But my mother gladly lights a candle on this day.

She says my father moving out was the best thing that could have happened to the family. To explain this a little, my father is a very strong minded person, and liked to control the entire family. He could be violent but not enough to cause marks, but it was the mental anguish he put my mother, my sister and myself through that was the worst. He would ask my mother why she did not put me 'away' somewhere. Why did he have to share his house with a drivelling fool, who could not even visit the bathroom without help? You will realise that I had severe disabilities and did indeed need help at all times, but this my mother gave willingly; and my mind was not slow, but it was very difficult to express myself.

My sister too suffered at his hands and from his tongue. She is in fact very intelligent, far more so than our father. He used to say she had ideas above her station and that a good hiding would soon get the ideas out of her head. My mother managed most times to stop this.

My mother, of course, took the brunt of his anger, which was more at the world than anything. He seemed to feel he should not be the only one going out to earn a living, and that my illness and disabilities were responsible for all the misfortunes that betook the family.

The day he left, telling my mother she could look after the fool and Lady Muck on her own, that we was off to someone who had time to look to his needs, it was as though the whole family relaxed. My mother used to say we began life that day.

My illnesses became more prevalent, and eventually my body could not fight any more and I came over to this world.

It's easier to communicate now, but not so easy for my sister to cope. My mother is very well adjusted. She tells everyone she is so grateful for the time we had together and that she regrets not one second of the time she spent looking after me; she is a fine woman.

My father says I should never have been born, and that my mother was no good as a breeder – she gave him no one to take to the match or the pub you see. But deep inside his thoughts a small voice stirs and now and again he wakes in the night.

I do not hate, dislike or resent my father. He is who he is; he has his own path to walk. I now walk mine gladly. My mother, now an elderly lady, walks hers with a good man. My sister is happy.

I send my love to all. God Bless

35. A Christmas Story

Do you want to hear a Christmas Story – MY Christmas story? Well first of all you have to know that when I was born my mother was quite elderly, she was nearly 40. The Doctors had told her that it may turn out that I had some medical problems because her body was getting a little old to be carrying a first child. My mother was prepared to take the risk, and I was born. It took a couple of years before anyone realised that I wasn't developing the same as other children my age. I could walk in a fashion, but didn't have much in the way of balance, and I could talk but never got past the baby talk when other children developed more natural speech. But my mother and my father loved me, spent hours with me, and never made me feel as though I was a burden, which I must have become as time went on, because I never became independent, and I never managed to attend a school. I did however have a lovely life, albeit a short one. When I was four I began having difficulty balancing at all, and before I was five I was confined to a wheelchair, and just after my fifth birthday I died. My mother was heartbroken, my father too, although he showed it in a different way. My mother cried and cried, my father simply went quiet.

My mother called to see a gentleman who tried to contact those of us in our world who wish to be contacted, but she was too soon, I was too young to be able to come and talk to him on my own, and the people who so lovingly cared for me did not think the time was right for me to talk to her. So my mother was disappointed. She kept on trying for a year or two, but then gave up all attempts, and declared to any who would listen, that she did not believe in an after life as I would never have abandoned her. I was at that time just before the time when I would have celebrated my seventh birthday.

At a time when, had I been still on earth, I would have become nine, I asked the people who cared for me if I could go and see my mother, and this time try to talk to her. I had been to visit several times, but had not been able to communicate, I had simply watched her and tried to show her I loved her, but my mother had not been able to recognise that I was there. This time I wanted to be more persuasive. They showed me several ways I could attract her attention. I learned to move the air a little so that it felt like I was kissing her cheek, I learned to move ornaments just a tiny bit, so that she would know she had been visited, and I learned to talk into her mind so that she would hear my voice.

All these attempts I tried when I came to visit, but my mother just thought there was a draught, that my father had been moving things, and most of all, that she was imagining things. I kept on trying, and I kept on failing, to let my mother know that I was there.

A friend of my mother had visited a lady who had the ability to join the two worlds together, and I was able to give her a message to give to my mother. She passed the message on, in every word, saying that she had been told of a child who was growing in the Spirit World, whose mother's name was Vera, and whose own name was Josie. My mother was interested but could not bring herself to trust the message, thinking that her friend was simply trying to comfort her. She did decide secretly however, to seek out a different person herself, to try and see if anything happened. I had told her friend that if my mother would try I would give her some proof.

It was by now November, and nearing ten years since I had been born. My mother made an appointment for the day of my birthday, but told no one, not even my father, that she was going to do this. She duly turned up, very nervous, and very sceptical. She was sure she would be disappointed and would not let herself hope that I would communicate.

During her time with the gentleman who was a communicator, she was given messages from my grandmother who was her own mother, and from her older brother, both of whom I knew well, and who visited my mother and also came to give me support as I grew. She accepted this evidence, but it was clear that was not what she was wanting to hear. My uncle gently pushed me forward so that I could talk myself. First of all I said that I was called Josie and wanted to give a message to my mother. The gentleman passed this information on, and then, when my mother gasped, I said that her name was Vera, and then I said that my father's name was Joe, which was why I was called Josie. At this point my mother started to cry. I sent her lots of love feelings, and the man passed them on to her, and then I started trying to talk into my mother's mind. She could not take it in so I talked to the man instead. It was a very emotional time for all of us, my grandmother, my uncle, myself and of course my mother. I did manage to give her one or two things that made her smile, and afterward she told the man that he had given her hope to carry on.

So I did manage to talk to her after all. But what I really wanted was for my mother to accept that I was around her quite a lot, which she had never done. One morning she woke up and smiled, and said to my father, "I think Josie is with us today". To be truthful I wasn't there at that time, but I picked up the love that she sent to me and I did come to see her that morning. She was preparing a meal for herself and my father, and was going to great pains to make sure everything was perfect. As she was preparing the vegetables I said in her ear, "Yuck sprouts I don't want any". She laughed and I knew she had heard me. And then she realised what she had done and heard and she said "Josie is that you?" I laughed and she heard that too, and rushed in to my father with tears rolling down her face, she was laughing and crying together. I just sent lots of love to them both and then stayed with them for a lot of the day. My mother wanted to lay a place for me at the table, but my father laughed and said no because everyone who ate at the table had to eat sprouts. He sort of winked inside his mind, so that I knew he was sending me love.

So that was my Christmas story, when my mother finally accepted that I really was talking to her and that I really did still come to see her and still love her. She doesn't always notice when I am there but she does sometimes so that is good isn't it?

(17th December 2006)

36 Amadeus

Thank you for giving me this chance to tell my tale.

I was born into your world for a very short time.

My mind would have worked with no problem, but my body would not have managed to work without a great deal of help from the medical teams. I would also have needed a great deal of money used to keep my body working. I would not have been able to run, jump, skip, hop or simply walk. Indeed I would not have been able to sit up or feed myself.

I have no recollection of living in your world, but I have many lovely memories of my childhood in the realm I now inhabit.

As a very young spirit I was cared for by a team of both men and women who devote their lives to helping young spirits to start on their path of development.

Does that seem odd to you? That we develop in this world? We need to develop our minds and our experiences just as you do on earth. We could be of no help to you if we did not understand pain, or sorrow, or anger or fright, or to recognize that what we normally feel is love and happiness. Our normal way of living is to enjoy experiencing new things as often as possible as children or young spirits. We come to your world to experience the difference; and how different it is and yet how similar.

We have no need to sleep, or to eat, or to wash, or to work manually. We do not need to learn to walk or learn to speak. We do not speak as you do, but we communicate very easily. We learn from an early age to recognize those who care for us just as a baby in your world learns to trust. We learn to ask with our minds. We think to the person and they hear us and think the answer back. We do not think, and everyone around us hears; that would be very confusing.

When I reached a certain stage, that is when I could understand what was happening and had a little confidence in myself; and when I could reach out in my mind to ask questions and receive answers; I transferred to a larger group where I remained until I was old enough to live my life – not without help, we always need and give that from and to each other, but independently enough to move to the next stage of my development or progression you may wish to call it.

It has often been said that when we decide to spend a part of our existence helping those of your world, or bringing up those spirits who come to us at an early age, that we put our progression on hold. Technically that is correct but in reality how quickly would we progress if we did not seek to help others?

If we spent our entire time learning we would certainly eventually progress, but how can you become pure Spirit and move to become part of the energy if we have no love or compassion for others?

I would certainly have missed learning a great deal about your world, and missed great opportunities to study and to understand the people, the spirits, who come to our world having spent many, many years in your own.

It can be very confusing to try and understand the reasons behind the actions of some in your world. Those who take a delight in seeing others suffer; those who do not treasure their children, indeed those who make the lives of the precious young spirits in their care miserable or even unbearable. It is necessary to study these people to see what has made them behave the way that they do, as without understanding there can be no realistic help for them.

That is how I now spend my existence. I will not say time for time as you understand it does not exist in our world.

At some stage I may be able to help one or more of the individuals to live a more worthwhile life, and not to depend upon acts which would be impossible to imagine in my world. I hope so. At the moment I am learning and studying as much as I can.

Does it seem strange to you that I spend my time helping such as these rather than the ones you would call their victim? But you see, unless you stop the action from the source it will continue. A stream does not stop flowing because you divert its path, it merely moves in another direction. I do not presume to know the answers yet, indeed I may never do so, but I feel I must try.

Thank you for letting me put across my view, and thank you for being patient. May the blessings of your world be felt stronger and stronger as you continue with your own progression.

Goodbye and enjoy your time on your world.

Amadeus (or Abdias I am not sure)

37. Amelia (?)

My Mummy came to your world to meet me. It was very brave of her because she had not had a happy time when she was living there herself. She had been beaten often by my father and when I was three years old she was beaten so badly that she did not live.

My brother did his best to look after me, and comfort me, but in truth he was only eight himself.

My father was appalled at my mother's passing, but never really accepted that it was his fault. He did not consider himself a bad person, he treated my mother as his father had dealt with his mother.

I was not a strong child, and my father did not know how to care for me. He usually sent my brother to buy food but as I say my brother was too young for the responsibility. He did not give me the food a growing child needs, although it did fill my belly.

Eventually I was taken ill and, because my body was not well nourished, I grew more and more weak. One night I was in my bed and trying to be quiet as my father always insisted, but I was coughing and coughing. Eventually I choked and as I did so I saw my mother at my side.

As any child would I held out my arms to be comforted and my mother picked me up and held me.

She carried me with her and we came to where it got lighter and brighter and warmer and warmer. Oh how good that warmth felt. My bed I had just left was cold, and to be truthful not always dry. I felt full suddenly – no longer hungry and no longer cold and frightened.

My mother told me how much she loved me and how much she missed me and how glad she was to have me near her.

I did not stay with my mother all the time. I lived with other children so that we could learn together but I saw my mother often.

I also came many times to see my brother and indeed my father. My brother grew strong but also his heart hardened towards my father. He left home as soon as he could and has had very little contact with my father since then. He did well for himself and worked hard. He now has a wife and a child of his own and is very, very careful that his little boy always knows love and kindness.

I grew up with fun and laughter, learning to play and to share happiness. My mother is now settled and happy with her friends and her family around her.

My father? He married again, but this time the woman he married was strong enough to refuse to accept the treatment. He spent time in prison and was given, and thankfully accepted, counselling. I would not say he is now completely changed, but he is calmer now.

So my family is separated, but in our own ways we are happier and we live better lives then we did together.

Do I have regrets? No, but I do have feelings of love and support for my family, and for all those I come in contact with. I do not regret coming to this world earlier than would have seemed likely, for I have had a much more fulfilling time than I would had I stayed on your earth. I am happy.

12th August 2007

I was not given a name, but a lady in the Church where I read this the day it came to me told me afterwards she felt that her name was Amelia

Part 2
The Poems

1   Hello Mummy

I came back to see you today Mummy
Did you know that I ruffled your hair?
I saw you play games with the cat Mummy
Did you know that I visit you there?

You were sad when you stood by my bed Mummy
I picked up your thoughts as I played
You wished that I'd lingered with you Mummy
But I would have had pain if I'd stayed

I came to where flowers are bright Mummy
Where children are happy and free
I don't have to wear hospital gowns Mummy
I'm not ill anymore as you see

You wonder what I'm doing now Mummy
You would have a surprise if you knew
We went to see animals play Mummy
And then I rode on a Gnu

I walk and I skip and I jump Mummy
My friends and I laugh and have fun
We don't have any tears over here Mummy
But best of all – now I can run

Please hang bright balloons on your walls Mummy
Don't think of how I used to be
This Christmas remember good times Mummy
And know that much love comes from me

2 I Live A Life So Pure

I live a life so pure and free
I wish to let you share with me
I travel here I travel there
I can go just anywhere

I'm in your thoughts
I'm in your mind
I'm in your heart
I'm in your soul
I'm in your every movement

Remember just as you love me
I love you always mother
I want to let you know so much
I love you like no other

I'm in your thoughts
I'm in your mind
I'm in your heart
I'm in your soul
I'm in your every movement

My father too is my best friend
He has a place so special
He wonders how my life is now
Please tell him time is precious

I'm in your thoughts
I'm in your mind
I'm in your heart
I'm in your soul
I'm in your every movement

3   *I Am Here*

You ask where I am
I am here
You ask "are you there?"
I am here
You ask "where are you now"
I am here

You want to know what I do
You want to know what I see
You want to know what I hear
You want to know what I feel

I do what is best for me
I see all around the sea
I hear all the birds so free
I feel all the love you send

You want to know what I do
You want to know what I see
You want to know what I hear
You want to know what I feel

I do all that I want to do
I see all I want to see
I hear all I want to hear
And I feel all the love you feel
I am here

4   *We Come To See You*

We come to see you we come to call
We come to tell you we didn't die at all
We simply moved from there to here
It's just a different hemisphere

What more can we say
What more can we write
What more do you need
Way into the night

You need to know
And we need to say
We love you more
With each passing day

Love did not stop
When our earth's heart stilled
The heart that loves
Is forever filled

The world's heart beats
The Universe lives
With all the energy
That your precious love gives

5   *Can I Sit By Your Side*

Can I sit by your side and stroke your hair,
as you stroked mine before?
Can I watch you bake with that warm kitchen glow?
I used to feel before?
Can I hold your hand as in days now gone?
and feel the comfort there?
Can I look in your eyes
and see the love
that never went away?

Can I sit on your lap
as you read a book?
Can I lie in my bed
as you snuggle me in?
Can I smuggle the cat
beneath the sheets
as I used to do before?

6   *Remember*

Remember please as you lay down to rest
The memories you hold dear
Are the same for me in our separate worlds
Which run side by side through life's test

Each time you see my face in your mind
Each time I smile in your heart
Each time you see me standing there
Are the times when we're not apart

Each moment we shared is in our precious store
Each second will one day be shared
Each game and each smile
And even each frown
Are the times we both know that we cared.

7   I Was Nine

I was 9. I was ill
I kept throwing out my pill
I held fast to my mother
I wanted no other
She cried when she thought I was sleeping

She held me she nursed me
She loved me she stroked me
She prayed nothing would hurt me
She wanted to cure me
And she cried when she thought I was sleeping

I went away to another place
I came to here with lots of space
No wheelchairs here
No sticks or steps - none needed
We don't cry we aren't sleeping.

My mother despairs because I'm not there
She thinks she did wrong some how somewhere
She can't see me – she tries
And then breaks down and cries
I wish she could see me not sleeping

(Given shortly before Mavis' Children's séance in 2004 – a series of short poems –these came through very quickly and I am not altogether sure where one poem ends and another begins, hence they are listed almost as one)

8   *There Are Lots Of Us Here*

There are lots of us here in this big bright world,
Some who lived in dark places on yours
There are lots of us here who weren't sickly
There are lots of us came very quickly

Give us this day our daily bread
Give us this day somewhere for my head
Give us the chance to come home on a night
To a home full of love and not fight.

That's how I prayed when I lived in your world
That's how I prayed as my body I curled
That's how I prayed every night of my life
As I lived in a world full of strife

One evening I looked and saw out in the night
A most beautiful lady all covered in light
She said if I went with her I really just might
Find that my prayers had come true

So I went and I found that the children were kind
They laughed and sang and loved
I was full and warm and dry

Please tell all the mothers our sorrow was THEN
We live in a world so bright like a gem
Don't be sad for us then
That time has passed
Just be glad for us now
As we love first and last.

We all want to come to your special event
Our mothers would love it to have time with us spent
We can't all be speakers
But watch for shoe 'tweakers'
and watch when we show you
how much we have fun

Children of our world unite
To talk to parents dear
To tell you that we live and love
And hold your memories here

We love you so
You need to know
Please feel the glow
As we try to show

They like us to laugh
They like us to learn
They like to be sure
That we feel whole and pure
That the pain of our past
has all faded at last

We travel all over
In your world and ours
We don't know of time
But we bet we've had hours
of fun with the animals
fun with the trees
fun with the ocean
and fun with the breeze

Don't all be sad for us
don't all be blue
just smile as you think of what we get to do
We love you we miss you
We want you to know
The more smiles you send us the more love will flow

It isn't just mothers
Our fathers grieve too
Sometimes they are strong
but sometimes it breaks through
We know what they feel
We know what they say
Remember, we feel it
each time that you pray.
Remember our love
Remember our joy
Remember the good times
With your girl or boy.

Some of us were lost before we came to earth
Our bodies were broken but our souls had a worth
We came to a place where we needn't be ill
Where the sun shines all day and with good feeling we fill
We came to a place where we could grow tall
Where our bodies' afflictions don't hurt us at all

Don't call us back to our bodies so frail
You would never be happy while we looked so pale
We came to where everything is so pure
It's more than was prayed for. It's more than a cure.

There are those of you out there
Wanting to shout
'My loss wasn't like that
My child was so bright
But because of bad people his life was wiped out'

I wanted to tell you what happened to me
I was there on your earth plain just playing and free
And then very quickly please don't ask me how
I came to this place to the here and the now
I don't feel the pain and I don't have the fright
That wakens my parents long into the night
Please help them to know that I'm happy to say
There are lots here who love me and show me the way
We all want to tell you however we came
Through illness or accident it all counts the same
We have in our memories sweet moments with you
Please share those with us and know love that is true.

9   *Keep A Place For Me*

I don't need a big place
I don't ask for much
I don't need a fireside
it won't cost you as such

Just keep me a place
in your loving heart
and always remember
of your family I'm still part

10 Hi Mummy Hi Daddy I Love You

Hi Mummy Hi Daddy I love you
I bet you don't know where I am
I just sat astride a young ostrich
and talked to a big fat old clam!

I think of you doing the shopping
and driving around place to place
With Dad getting cross with the traffic
and Mum with that look on her face

But then I see both of you sitting
and lovingly wishing me well
I used to pretend to be sleeping
then shock you by giving a yell!

Sometimes I come with you on car trips
I don't need a belt anymore
I can jump the way you used to stop me
but I know that's 'cos I got so sore

I wish you could see me just running
and not having to stop for a rest
I haven't got pain in my legs now
and I don't need my sticks that's the best

I have a nice lady looks over me
she says I'm a very nice boy
She says you must be lovely parents
'cos you helped me to have lots of joy

My friends all came with me last Tuesday
we played with the cat and the dog
We laughed when you saw them run round, Dad
you thought they were scared by the fog

There's a baby who soon will be with you
he's not a replacement for me
He's going to be one on his own Mum
and as he grows up he'll see me

He's going to be one of the people
who break down the barriers see?
He'll help lots of others gain comfort
by showing their loved ones are free

Well be able to talk to you through him
he may even let you talk to me
Keep knowing that I'll always be here
'cos that's how it's all meant to be

11   I Wish That's How It Was

Why did I have to leave you?
It wasn't an idea of mine
I couldn't have stayed if I'd tried
And how do you think it would work
I was sick and frail and tired
And getting more ill by the day

Perhaps there was some plan
To desert you and go on my own
To have fun while you do so much
To bring children up by yourself
If there was it was no plan of mine
I longed to stay with you all the time

I can see you and hear you from here
I can visit whenever I want
I can put thoughts in the back of your mind
And read what you think of your life
If the children play up I would help
But you can't change a nappy from here.

You can't hug a child fallen out of a tree
Or pick him up and send him back home
It isn't the unallied joy that I thought
And I can't change my mind and come back
But it beats all those needles and syringes
And I don't have to take pills any more

I wish in some ways it was different
I wish it was just as it was
Before I was struck by the 'lurgy'
And had to submit to those tests

I know how hard it is for you dear
But don't think I could do anything else

I hear you shout out at midnight
"How could you have left me this way?
How could you have gone when I need you?
And now I'm left all on my own?"
Please darling I wouldn't go lightly
And I'd come straight back if I could.

My anger's not all dissipated
They say it gets calmer with time
But now it's raw and I hate them
They love me and tell me I'm fine
They say that we all have gone through it
And I'll love and help others quite soon.

I wish I could say something different
I wish I could hold you again
They say I will soon be much better
And settle to my new life well
I feel so frustrated and futile
But somehow I think they are right

It's so soon since I passed over to here Dear
Perhaps we will both soon adjust
The anger will go from us both Dear
If only we give ourselves time
Please always remember I love you
And its not want I wanted to do.

(The poem on the next page is from the same young man – about nine months later)

12 *It's Getting Better*

I saw you today in the garden
You were hanging the clothes on the line
And just for an instant you felt me
Now I know you are going to be fine.

You hug the kids to you and whisper
"I love you and Daddy does too"
They hardly remember when waking
But sleeping they see me so well.

"If only" I here you so often
But life didn't turn out that way
I needed to come here my Darling
You know how I wanted to stay.

We each have a role now to play dear
You feed, clothe and comfort so well
I'll guide and support and advise dear
You pick my thoughts up clear as a bell.

13 I'll Be There

On your big family day – I'll be there
When the family's together - I'll be there
When you love and laughter share
When you gather anywhere
One thing is very sure - I'll be there

When you think I'm missing out - I'll be there
When you want to sing and shout - I'll be there
When the happiness is glowing
And your love for all is showing
Never fear that I won't notice - I'll be there

When you take the dog for walks – I'll be there
When your good times rise like larks – I'll be there
When the sun is shining bright
And you feel the world's just right
That's the time I love the best - I'LL BE THERE!

14 *Keep Me In Your Heart But Let Me Go*

Keep me in your heart but let me go
I need to spread my wings and learn to grow
Help me leave this wasted body lie
And let my soul go soaring towards the sky

Keep me in your mind but let me go
You know I'll always love you – let me go
Don't hold me back to suffer night and day
Let me go and live a better way

Keep me in your thoughts but let me go
Hold the good times close but let me go
Remember when we loved and laughed and smiled
And always know that I am free at last

15 Forever

What do I wish more than ever?
I wish for you to go on and live as I do
Forever

What do I want from life?
I want everything to be clean and fresh
Forever

What do I want you to know?
I want you to know I'm alive and loving you
Forever

What do I need right now?
I need your laughter to rise up and spread
Forever

2nd October 2004

16 Has Anyone Reminded You?

Has anyone reminded you how much I love you?
Has anyone reminded you how much I care?
Has anyone thought to tell you I am waiting here?
Till the day I know you realise I'm there

I want to get a feeling of my new life
I want to get a feeling of what's new
I want to know that you will help yourself now
And find a life that's happy for you too

You spent so long in helping me
You spent so long in trying
You spend your days just missing me
I hate to see you crying

Please help me now and help yourself
Please help me see you through this
Please help to let me live in peace
And send your loving blowing kiss

2nd October 2004

17 *How Can I Be Dead?*

How can I be dead? I'm talking to you now
How can I be dead I'm more alive than ever
How can I be dead? I can see you here and now
How can I be dead? I'm not – I'm just a feather

I can laugh and I can smile
I can jump and run a mile
I can float as free as air
And I can see you sitting there.

I had a will to live
I had a will to stay
I had a will to love
And I had a will to play

I asked the pain to go
I asked the pain to stop
I asked that I be well
And I asked to play and not drop

They answered me

The pain has gone
The pain has stopped
I am well
I do not drop

2nd October 2004

18 *I Am Not Alone*

No one tells me what to do, but I am not alone
No one tells me how to sit, but I am not alone
Now one makes me milk the cow
Or clean the barn or feed the sow
But never do I ever feel alone

Someone holds my hand; I know I'm not alone
Someone helps me understand that I am not alone
Someone helps me feel at home
They help me grow they help me know
And never do I ever feel alone

You wonder how I manage on my own
You wonder if I'm frightened on my own
You wonder if they help me
Hold me and protect me
You wonder if I'm left here on my own

They love me and I'm never on my own
They teach me how to know I'm not alone
They nurture me and keep me safe
They hold me close this little waif
And never am I ever all alone.

19 Relax

Relax; relax its going to be fine
Sit back, put your feet up, make that chair recline
Don't be so worried
Don't be so hurried
Don't be afraid to let life take its time
I know how you feel about stopping to think
But try to remember
Although it's December
I don't want my death to bring you to the brink
Relax, relax, and remember I'm here
Don't think I've abandoned you
Don't live with that fear
Pick up the kitten, just sit back and listen
I'm only a breath away I am so near
I'm here in your heart
We're not truly apart
Put down the cleaner
Put down the brush
Turn off the music
Enjoy the hush
And please do remember my Spirit lives on
It's only my weakened ill body that's gone
Relax, relax don't doubt that it's me
The only thing different? Of pain I am free
The tumour is gone
But my humour lives on

Please smile that's my order or at least my plea
Remember, remember it's my wish that you feel
The greatest of love sent to help you to heal
Accept what's given it isn't so hard
At the end of the rainbow there is a reward
The tears soon will dry
Your soul once again fly
And then you will realise
My love is still real

About the Author

Karen lives on the North East coast of England and is proud to call herself a Yorkshire woman. Born and bred in Yorkshire, she spent many years living in Berkshire before returning to the North East in 2000.

She developed as a medium in a Church circle and has taken Church services in many parts of the Country.

The poetry started arriving in 1994, with the stories beginning shortly afterwards, but although they were read out in Churches, with a good reception, Karen was unsure what to do with them. Over the next ten years she was frequently advised to have them published. In between working full time, continuing to work as a medium, still taking Church services, and leading a busy social life, the book has slowly come together.

Recently turned 60 Karen is now hoping to enjoy a quieter life, spending more time with her partner, and with her two cats. It is possible this may not be as easy as she would like, as the pieces and poems continue to arrive.

Printed in the United Kingdom
by Lightning Source UK Ltd.
131505UK00002B/1-54/A